Industrial Studies

A coursebook for economic, industrial, commercial and 'understanding industry' courses

Alan Jamieson

Edward Arnold

© Alan Jamieson 1986

First published in Great Britain 1986 by
Edward Arnold (Publishers) Ltd, 41 Bedford Square,
London WC1B 3DQ

Edward Arnold (Australia) Pty Ltd, 80 Waverley
Road, Caulfield East, Victoria 3145, Australia

British Library Cataloguing in Publication Data

Jamieson, Alan,
   Industrial studies: a coursebook for economic,
industrial, commercial and 'understanding industry'
courses.
1. Great Britain — Industries
I. Title
338.0941   HC256.6

ISBN 0-7131-7498-6

All rights reserved. No part of this publication may
be reproduced, stored in a retrieval system, or
transmitted in any form or by any means,
electronic, photocopying, recording, or otherwise,
without the prior permission of Edward Arnold
(Publishers) Ltd.

Text set in 10/11 pt Univers Medium Compugraphic
by Colset Private Limited, Singapore.
Printed and bound by The Bath Press, Avon.

Contents

Who is this book for?		v
How to use the book		v
The company		**1**
1	Industry, commerce and business	1
2	Starting up	5
3	Forming a business	7
4	The idea	11
5	Research, product planning and development	13
6	Market research, or who'll buy what we're selling	15

Expanding the firm		**18**
7	Pricing, or can you make a profit?	18
8	Going after the money	21
9	'Shall we go public?'	24
10	Case-studies	28

Industry and commerce		**32**
11	The location of industry	32
12	Manufacturing industry	35
13	Marketing	43
14	Advertising	46
15	Selling	52
16	Company case-studies	58
17	Multinational companies	60

Suppliers and consumers		**62**
18	Supply and demand	62
19	More turnover and bigger profits	64
20	Protecting the consumer	67

People at work		**72**
21	The individual at work	72
22	Labour relations	78
23	Employers' associations	84
24	Employee participation	86

Government and business		**92**
25	Private and public sectors	92
26	Public spending	96
27	Energy, pollution and conservation	100
28	Personal incomes . . . and how they are spent	106
29	Money and inflation or how the government seeks to control the economy	111
30	Projects	114
Index		**117**

Acknowledgements

The publishers would like to thank the following for their permission to include copyright material:

The Forestry Commission p. 4 (top left)
Barclays Bank plc p. 4 (top right)
British Petroleum Co plc p. 4 (bottom left)
Ford Photographic Library p. 4 (bottom right)
Companies Registration Office p. 9
Birds Eye Wall's Limited p. 10
Philips p. 10
Tesco p. 10
TrainLines of Britain and Wella Great Britain p. 10
Wellcome p. 10
Rolls-Royce Ltd Bristol/Arthur Kemsley p. 14
Apple Computer (UK) Ltd p. 24
The Stock Exchange p. 25
Times Newspapers Ltd/David Lavender pp. 28 & 31
Ann Hills p. 29
Panasonic UK Ltd p. 33
Peterborough Development Corporation p. 34
Management Today (Sandy Porter)/Nabisco Ltd p. 36 (top)
Camera Press p. 36 (bottom)
Mullard Southampton p. 37
Management Today/Armatron p. 38
Northumberland County Council p. 41
Halifax Building Society p. 46
Heinz p. 46
Penguin p. 46
Ziebart p. 46
Struthers Advertising and Marketing Ltd p. 48
Horizon Holidays p. 49
Spar (UK) Ltd p. 54 (top)
The Burton Group plc p. 54 (bottom)
John Lewis Partnership p. 55 (left)
Tesco Training Services p. 55 (right)
J Sainsbury plc p. 56 (top)
The Littlewoods Organisation Ltd p. 56 (bottom)
Marks and Spencer plc p. 58
Esso Petroleum Co Ltd p. 61
Elida p. 63
BEAB p. 68
British Standards Institution p. 68
The Design Council p. 68
The Advertising Standards Authority p. 69
British Furniture Manufacturers p. 69
Home Laundering Consultative Council p. 69
National Inspection Council for Electrical Installation Contracting p. 69
American Express Europe Ltd p. 70
Her Majesty's Stationery Office p. 75
BBC Hulton Picture Library p. 79
Philip Walmuth p. 82
James Holmes p. 84
Reed International p. 90
British Broadcasting Corporation p. 92
Birmingham City Council p. 92
The Electricity Council p. 92
Manpower Services Commission p. 92
Hertfordshire County Council p. 99
UK Atomic Energy Authority p. 100
National Society for Clean Air/C H Wood p. 101
Imperial War Museum p. 103

Who is this book for?

This book has been written to give information to, and to develop skills for, students who need to understand the contemporary economic, industrial and commercial structure of Britain. It will also help them to form their own opinions about business life, and to be better able to assess the opinions of other people.

Objectives

In particular, the book should help students to:
1 Know about the organisation of companies and businesses and to appreciate the motivation of people who start up in business *or* who are employed within large companies and organisations.
2 Understand the function and work of owners, managers, employees, trade unionists, consumers and citizens, and to appreciate the possible conflicts of interest between these roles.
3 Know about the impact of government on industrial, commercial and regional life, and to be able to assess the implications of government policy for private citizens.
4 Assess for themselves the pattern of relationships within industrial and commercial structures, and so help them to judge the impact and influence of information and opinions provided through the media and other sources.
5 Develop skills in communicating their own viewpoints on these topics, and express information and ideas through written, oral and other work.

Courses

The book has been planned to fit several courses and syllabuses. Among them are:
- GCSE courses on industry, commerce and business.
- The industrial, social and economic core studies element of the Certificate of Pre-Vocational Education (CPVE).
- Industrial Studies and similar schemes within City and Guilds foundation courses and the general studies element of craft and technician courses.

It will also be useful for other pre-vocational schemes in schools and further education colleges which are concerned with the transition to working life.

How to use the book

This book contains:
- *information* on a range of different topics concerned with industry and commerce.
- *assignments, questions and exercises* spread throughout the text.
- *discussion exercises* to enable students in small groups to share ideas.
- *projects* which help students to study a subject in some depth, giving them opportunities to present information in various ways and to communicate ideas in written and illustrative forms.

This lively and interesting way of working should help students to understand the information, to develop skills of communication and to form their own attitudes on subjects that will concern them as citizens.

The company

1
Industry, commerce and business

We shall start this book, as you should start any school or college course, by asking 'What *is* industry, commerce and business?', 'What do these words *mean*?'.

Let's begin with what you know. In the newspapers, and on radio and television, you will read, listen to or watch news stories concerned with daily events. Many of the stories are about business.

Here, for example, are eight typical news items. All eight of them are contained in the cartoon on this page. Which stories are connected closely with industry or commerce?

1 A strike in the docks leaves holiday-makers stranded.
2 Workers at a power station accidentally pollute a river.
3 A building society offers savers ten per cent interest.
4 A new motorway is opened between Watford and Wimbledon.
5 Hazel Jones, aged 18, opens her third hairdressing salon.
6 Shoppers queue to buy Hong Kong-made designer jeans at £5 a pair.
7 Farmers harvest a record crop of apples.

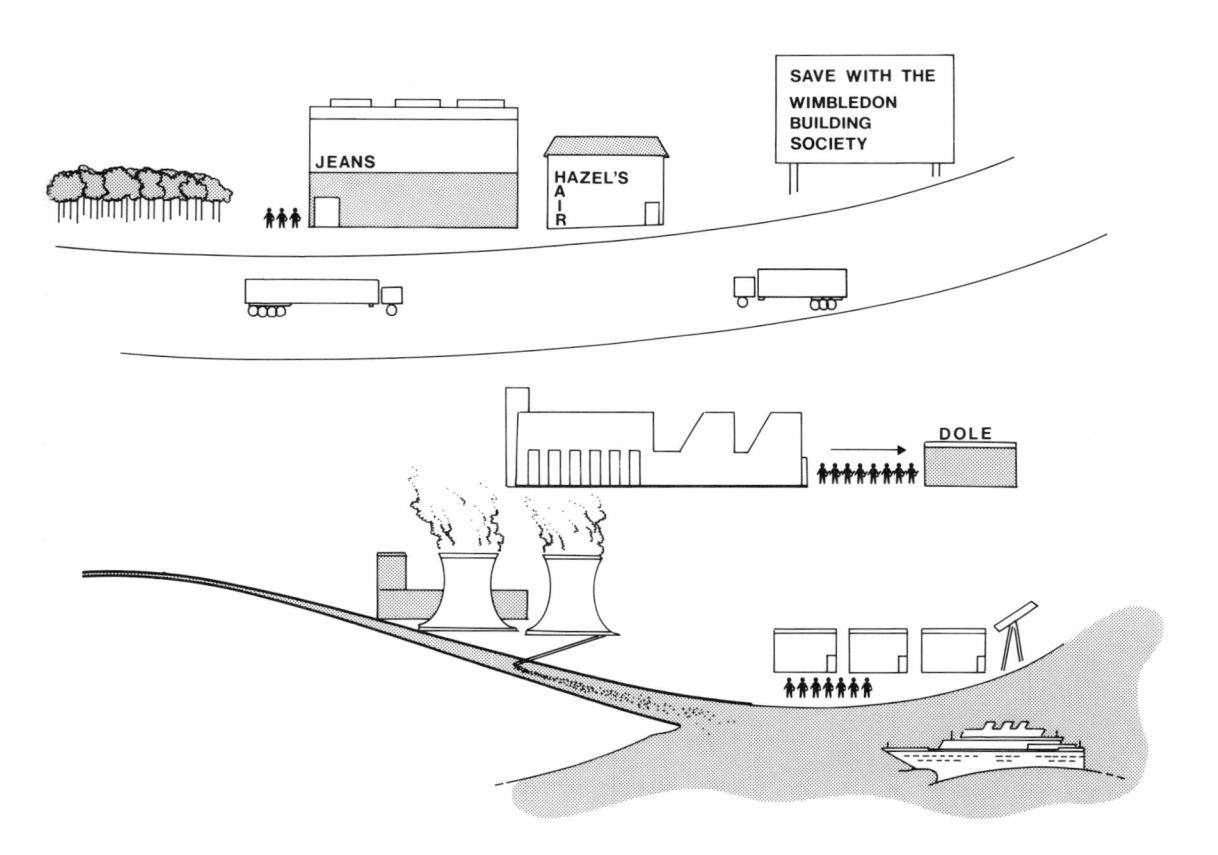

8 A factory closes with the loss of a thousand jobs.

The answer is – all of them. Each one is concerned with a company or organisation which produces something, which provides a service, which employs people. Each one involves money-making (or money-losing) and every one affects people – workers, managers, investors, consumers.

The next time you watch the news on television, list the number of stories which involve industry, commerce and business. You'll probably be surprised to find that almost every news item is on your list. Television itself is an industry. Every TV advert is part of someone's business. And, someone, somewhere, is buying and selling in order to make these enterprises work.

Industry . . . and you

When you begin work for the first time after leaving school, college or your training scheme, you are likely to be *employed*. It is possible, of course, that you could be *self-employed*, that is, have your own business. Or you may not be able to get a job, and be *unemployed*. Whatever your circumstances you'll be involved in industry or commerce. The reason is that people (whether they have a job or not) are part of the greatest resource used by the business world – the country's labour force.

Now it is time to have some definitions and to answer some questions.

Industry is a system for making or manufacturing things.

1 Name three different industries.

Commerce is the exchange of goods or money between individuals or countries.

2 Name three companies you know of which are engaged in commerce.

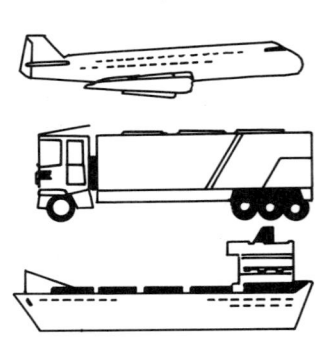

Business is the whole process of manufacturing, buying, trading and supply including banking and financial services.

3 Name three companies or organisations concerned with the business of:
(a) banking.
(b) insurance.
(c) housing.

Types of industry

You should now have a clearer idea about industry and commerce – what it *is* and what it *does*.

The experts divide industry into three main groups.

1 *Primary or extractive* industries produce raw materials or extract ores and include the coal, oil and iron industries. Farming and fishing are other important primary industries.

2 *Secondary or manufacturing* industries are concerned with making things. These could be complete items such as cars, washing machines, cookers, computers and so on, or they could be parts or *components* of these products – such as tyres, engines, heaters, circuits etc. Another section is the *assembly* industry where different parts are put together to make a complete product.

3 *Service* industries don't manufacture products but provide a service to *consumers* or to other industries. In this group are shops, garages, printers, hairdressers. You should be able to think of many more services. Ones which may not occur to you but which are important for the country's welfare are education (schools, universities); health (hospitals, doctors); libraries and many more 'social' services.

Consumers and producers

All of these companies and organisations have to produce something or provide a service which people want. It is no good making things or offering a service that no one will buy.

We are all *consumers*. We buy food and other goods which others provide. *This* is the *market* which companies aim to satisfy. Manufacturing and extraction businesses are *producers*, which means they make things that the consumers need or want. The service industries have a product too, but it's not always something you can see or handle. It might be documents (such as insurance), security, a personal service (such as that of an undertaker), or transport (taxis, buses, aeroplanes).

Commerce

Commerce is a term that needs a little more explanation.

There are six main groups of commercial businesses or organisations.
1 *Trading* – the buying and selling of goods, both within your own country and abroad.
2 *Warehousing* – the storage of goods until they are required for sale.
3 *Transport* – the road, sea, river, air and other links between producers and customers.
4 *Banking and finance* – the complex system of payment for goods in this country and abroad, loans, investment etc.
5 *Insurance* – compensation for damage to or the loss of goods, materials or services, and compensation for injury or loss.
6 *Advertising* – providing the consumers with information about goods for sale.

It is possible to put all this into a diagram which you could copy into your notebook, adding extra information such as:
- some examples of 'services' in the third main column.
- any other 'helps to business' which you can think of.
- some examples of 'assembly' industries.

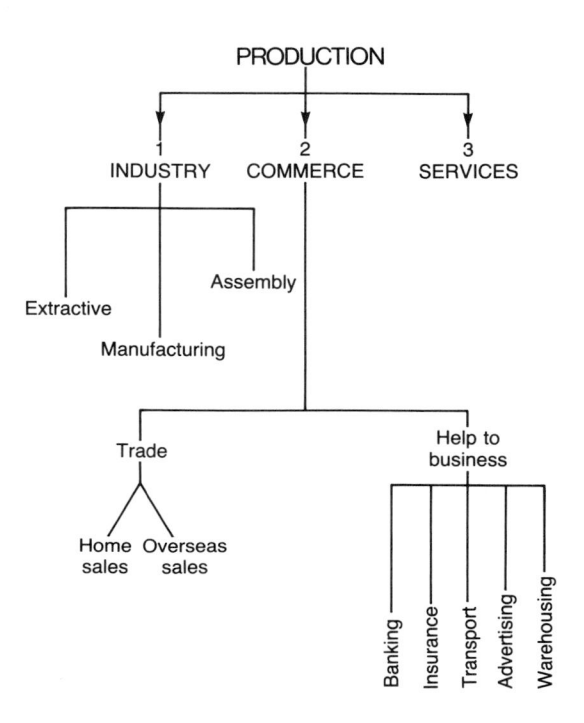

```
                    PRODUCTION
          ┌─────────────┼─────────────┐
          1             2             3
       INDUSTRY     COMMERCE       SERVICES
       ┌────┴────┐
              Assembly
   Extractive
       Manufacturing

           Trade                    Help to
                                    business
       ┌────┴────┐          ┌───┬───┬───┬───┬───┐
    Home    Overseas     Banking Insurance Transport Advertising Warehousing
    sales    sales
```

What are they?

Here is a test of your understanding so far. Match the photographs over the page to the four classes of industry.
1 Primary (extractive).
2 Primary (raw materials).
3 Secondary (manufacturing).
4 Service industry.

New industries

In Britain today, about 25 million people work in industry and commerce. The proportion of people in the service industries is increasing, as the number in primary and manufacturing industry falls. Most *new* businesses are also in the service sector, too. To start up a new company or product in a primary industry needs a great deal of money (*capital*) which only the massive companies such as Shell, BP, ICI, and the government can invest.

It is easier to make a start in a manufacturing business such as designing and making clothes, or car parts, or electronics. Capital is still needed, of course, to hire and equip a factory or

(a)

(b)

(c)

(d)

workshop, and the owners need to have brilliant ideas that no one has yet thought of in order to make a new product attractive to customers.

Most new businesses are in the service industries – hotels, shops, repairs, window-cleaning, hairdressing, and so on.

Your own book

As you work through this book, you should keep your own folder or workbook. Give it the title: Industrial Studies.

For a start write the answers to these

questions neatly in your book.

Questions

1 A group of people living together is called a *society*. The society in which we live is an *advanced industrial* society. But no matter where we live – whether it is in Britain, Africa, the Far East – there are five basic human needs. These are:
- food
- shelter
- clothing
- heat
- light

In your book, write a sentence to explain one way by which each of these was provided:
(a) 2500 years ago (that is, in the Stone Age).
(b) today, in an industrial society.

2 Write a sentence to explain each of these words or phrases:
- consumers
- manufactured goods
- service industries

2
Starting up

The *safe way* to learn about industry and commerce is to join a large company or organisation. There you can find out about manufacturing, selling, finance and the thousand and one other things involved in business.

If you make a mistake, you might feel worried about this, but you won't lose a lot of your money. Nor will you have to worry about debts, paying other people, ordering, managing accounts, customers and many other problems.

That's why most people prefer to work for someone else rather than take all the risks of 'going it alone'.

The *difficult or dangerous way* of discovering how business works is to start up on your own. It's like leaving the cosy security of your home for the first time. There are many risks and difficulties. You might have to work alone. You might need to borrow money with all the worry that this brings. And, worse, after all the hassle, the business might fail. And yet, each year thousands of people start their own business. In this chapter we shall look at how some people have taken the plunge! By examining real-life examples, it is easier to explain some of the business terms which you will be studying and will come across in any kind of commercial job.

Take away pizzas

Patrick and Sarah were students together on a college catering course. When the course ended, Sarah joined a food manufacturing company which specialised in dairy products. Patrick went to work in a hotel where he did everything from receptionist to assistant manager.

Two years later, they met up again, when they both attended a conference to which they'd been sent by their companies.

One evening, sitting with Patrick in the bar, Sarah talked about how she'd like to set up her own business.

'Doing what?' asked Patrick.

'Well, one idea I've got is called "Take Away Pizzas",' she replied. 'There are other take away shops – fish and chips, Chinese, pies and so on. They seem to do well, so why shouldn't "Call in for Your Pizza" be a success, too?'

'How do you know it will work?' asked Patrick.

'I've done my homework, my market research,' Sarah answered. 'I visited a hundred houses in town, and asked if they would buy pizzas. Ninety-two people said "yes". It's not a large number of people but it's enough to base a business on.'

Monsters and big ones

To cut a long story short, they decided to give up their jobs, form a partnership, buy or rent a shop, and start up 'Take Away Pizzas'. After only a year, encouraged by the first results, they formed a limited company with three directors – Sarah, Patrick and a friend, Michael, an accountant.

Patrick immediately put into effect the organising, business and marketing skills which he'd learned at the hotel. They decided that at first they would specialise in three varieties of pizza. These would be offered as: 'Monsters' (whole pizzas), 'Big Ones' (half pizzas) and 'Slices'.

They decided packaging was very important, so they paid a designer to construct neat red, white and blue boxes, made for the three different pizza sizes. 'Take Away Pizzas' was in big letters on every box.

Sarah's job, at first, was to find suitable premises. She was lucky in being able to rent a derelict shop in a prominent position in the centre of a town. After the shop had been gutted, repaired, decorated and equipped with cooking equipment, they were ready to open. Sarah knew a member of a group which had a record in the charts, and she persuaded the band (all four of them) to come to the opening. Patrick broke the news to the local newspaper, and on the day of the Grand Opening, over two thousand people turned up. They didn't all buy pizzas but they certainly knew about the new shop!

At the start, expenses were very high. The equipment included fridge, ovens and special catering equipment. They had to meet the strict standards laid down by laws on health and safety and the sale of food. Patrick wrote, had printed and distributed 2000 leaflets, pushed through the letterboxes of local residents.

Without sufficient capital of their own, they had to borrow. The bank gave them a loan but at a high rate of interest. They also needed a solicitor, surveyor, builder and decorator. All of them cost money. They employed two part-time helpers: one of these was a cook who shared the pizza-making with Sarah and Patrick. They all had to take their share on the oven.

'We made mistakes,' said Sarah. 'For example, we paid more than we needed for equipment, furniture and ingredients. Now we ask for, and get, good discounts on everything we buy.'

'Another mistake,' Patrick added, 'was in the layout of the shop. The cooking area is too small. On the other hand, we made one very successful decision, for we put the ovens in the *front* of the shop, near the window, instead of out of the way at the back. Every night for weeks, we had a crowd watching us make pizzas. Some of them even came in to buy one!'

And what of the future?

'Sarah and I had some disagreements along the way, but we get on very well together. One thing we haven't regretted, and that's being your own boss. You are responsible for the success – or the failure.'

'And that includes working or thinking about pizzas for about 16 hours a day!' added Sarah, ruefully.

Their plan is to build up the business gradually. Already they have one or two promising contracts. For instance, a local company and the hospital are two big customers, each with a standing order for 50 pizzas at lunchtimes.

Patrick had the last word. 'That's what we are after – volume sales,' he said. 'Clearly, it's less effort to sell 50 pizzas to one customer than one pizza to 50 customers. The more we sell, too, the lower our costs, and that means better profits.'

Setting up a small business enterprise

The story of the start of Patrick and Sarah's business gives you a good idea of what is involved. Each of the main factors will be examined in this book.

Let's analyse the business aspects of *Take Away Pizzas Ltd*.

Answer these questions in your notebook or folder.

1 *The idea* What was it?
2 *The knowledge* What business experience and knowledge did Sarah and Partrick have?
3 *Research* What did they do to find out if there was a market for pizzas?
4 *Premises* What did they do about siting the business?
5 *Production* How did they produce their pizzas?
6 *The company* They started with one kind of business enterprise, and later converted it to another: what were the two types?
7 *Finance* Where did the money come from?
8 *Advertising and marketing* How was this done?

3
Forming a business

When you get your first job, you could join a small company, perhaps with twenty people working for it, owned by one person. Or, you could move into a large firm, with five hundred employees. Thirdly, you could find a job with a huge organisation, such as the National Health Service, British Rail or a supermarket chain like Tesco or Sainsbury, with thousands of employees.

In this book, we shall be looking closely at all of these different kinds of businesses. It is important at this stage to understand who owns them and how they are formed.

Let's start with three kinds of *ownership* which a self-starter in business could manage.

Sole trader

This is where the owner, acting alone, is responsible for running the whole business. He or she invests the start-up capital; is self-employed; and if any staff are taken on, is responsible for them. If the business borrows money, the owner is solely responsible for the debts. On the other hand, if it's a big success, he or she takes all the profits.

A big disadvantage of being a sole trader is that if the business collapses and the owner is bankrupt (that is he cannot pay his debts), the owner's house, its contents and any savings can be taken by the creditors (people or companies to whom the debts are owed).

Examples of this kind of business are shopkeepers (such as newsagents), cafe and restaurant owners, butchers and bakers, small garages, plumbers, repairers, hairdressers etc.

Over the page are drawings of two 'sole traders'.

To see if you have understood the meaning of this form of business organisation, draw a cartoon story about a self-starter. These episodes could be in it.

- Joan decides to start a business and borrows money to finance it. (. . . at the bank, from parents, from friends . . . ?)
- She buys equipment and rents premises. (. . . shop, workshop . . .?)
- She makes a success of it and enjoys all the profits.
- Or, the business fails and Joan loses everything. (. . . bicycle, tools . . .)

Partnership

The second kind of business is an *ordinary partnership*. This is formed when two or more people put in their money to form a joint enterprise. One kind of partnership is a husband and wife team. Another is where two friends join up to start a business on their own. A third is where a *sleeping* partner (that is, non-active) puts in money to give someone with ideas and perhaps make money from them. A fourth kind is where up to twenty people provide the capital. This is called a *limited partnership* and isn't much different from limited company (see below).

There could be more than two partners. A legal agreement isn't required by law, but it is wise to have one, for partners have been known to fall out! If there is an agreement on paper, and one of the partners decides to leave, the break-up is much easier to arrange.

If a partnership gets into financial trouble, all partners are responsible for the debts. As with a sole trader, their personal belongings including their homes could be sold to pay the debts. But if profits are made, they are distributed according to the terms of the partnership agreement.

Here are two kinds of partnership. Continue the list by thinking of others.
- a plumber and a bricklayer form a building partnership.
- a husband and wife join up with a neighbour to own a local shop.

Private limited company

The third method is to form a private limited company. These are usually 'family' firms. They stay 'private' to keep the business in the family, and have between two and fifty shareholders. The shares are not sold on the Stock Exchange. Such a company has what is called *limited liability* which means that if the firm goes bankrupt, the shareholders are not liable to have their *savings* seized to pay the debts. Their liability is limited to *what they invested in the company*. For example, if Mr A bought 100 £1 shares in his brother's company, and the firm goes bust, Mr A loses only the value of the shares.

Here are some other aspects of a limited company:
- a shareholder cannot transfer his or her shares to another person without the agreement of the other shareholders.
- each year the company must supply business information to the Department of Trade and Industry: this must include a copy of the company's accounts and a list of its assets, money invested and the shareholders' and directors' names.

We shall examine the business organisation of large companies later but you should know that a limited company can be formed
either as a *private* company where the shares are owned by a group of people (as few as two, as

many as fifty).
or as a *public* company where the shares are bought and sold openly on the Stock Exchange: the shares can be owned by individuals, by other companies, by pension funds and other investors.

Test yourself

Now test your knowledge and understanding of these types of business organisation by copying this chart into your notebook, and completing it.

Which of the three words given is correct? Underline the correct word.

1	A person who cannot pay business debts is	director shareholder bankrupt
2	One of the equal parts of a company's capital is the	debt share profit
3	In this organisation the capital can be invested by up to twenty people.	partnership limited company sole trader
4	In this organisation the owner's personal goods cannot be taken to pay debts.	partnership Stock Exchange limited company

Registering a company

This is done in accordance with the Acts of Parliament (the Companies Acts). Rules have been laid down about how a private company should be formed.
The main rules are these:
- the company is run by a board of directors and a company secretary. The minimum number of directors is one (in a private company).
- directors are voted into office by the shareholders at a general meeting.
- when a company is formed, a solicitor has to draw up two documents: (a) the 'memorandum of association' which explains the rules that the company will obey in its business dealings; and (b) the 'articles of association' which describes the voting powers of shareholders, directors and other matters concerned with the company's organisation.

The next stage in the formation of the company is that the memorandum and articles of association are sent to the *Registrar of Companies*. He or she issues a Certificate of Incorporation. Once this has been received by the company, it can start *trading*, that is, begin business dealings.

CERTIFICATE OF INCORPORATION

OF A PRIVATE LIMITED COMPANY

No. 1585650

I hereby certify that

EMBLEMFAME LIMITED

is this day incorporated under the Companies Acts 1948 to 1980 as a private company and that the Company is limited.

Given under my hand at Cardiff the 14TH SEPTEMBER 1981

Assistant Registrar of Companies

C.173

A certificate of incorporation for a private company

Lastly, all companies are required by the terms of the Companies Acts to send information each year to the Department of Trade and Industry, with details of the shareholders, directors and officers, and a statement of accounts.

Shares

A *share* is a fixed part of the capital of a company.

Many companies start up by issuing one hundred £1 shares and the directors buy all of them.

There are two main kinds of shares: *preference* shares and *ordinary* shares.

Preference shares have a fixed rate of interest. (let's say 7 per cent per annum) which must be paid in full before any dividend is paid to people holding ordinary shares.

Ordinary shares do not have a fixed rate of interest. Instead, shareholders get a division of the profits (if there are any) after all other claims have been paid in full.

Another word you will come across is *debentures*. These are payments or loans made to a company by investors. They have a fixed rate of interest like preference shares and the holders have the right to their interest before any payments are made to preference or ordinary shareholders.

Public limited company

So far, all the information has been about a *private* limited company.

A private limited company cannot offer its shares to the general public. A *public* limited company, on the other hand, can offer shares on the Stock Exchange. This is usually done in order to raise more capital. For example, Company X needs money to invest in more equipment. The directors decide to offer 100 000 shares at £1 each. These are sold on the Stock Exchange, and as it is a successful company, the 100 000 shares are quickly snapped up. This is called 'going public', and companies that are in this category have the letters 'plc' after their name. To take this step, the company must have minimum capital of £50 000. There are legal requirements, too, which need not concern us here.

Questions

1. Invent the name of a company you'd like to form and manage.
2. Explain the steps you'd need to take in order to register it.

4
The idea

It should now be clear that the main feature of starting up a new business is to think up an *idea* or discover a new *business opportunity*.

Most business ideas come about in one of these ways:
- a completely new product, such as a chocolate bar specially designed, made and marketed by a large food company.
- a fresh development of an existing product such as this year's model of a Ford or BL car.
- an idea for a service which is different from anything else, such as the take away pizza.
- a breakthrough in science or engineering, such as the body scanner which detects disease.
- a breakaway, where an employee thinks he or she could do the job better than the company for which they work.
- using a hobby – photography, dress-making, designing, gardening – to start up a small business.
- using existing knowledge and skills – typing, cooking, electronics, dancing.
- using professional skills to go-it-alone, such as an accountant, estate agent, surveyor, solicitor and so on: these people will have spent a long time acquiring qualifications and experience before they set up on their own.
- buying an on-going business such as a hotel, garage or shop and making it into personal concern.

You should be able to think of other ways of setting up in business. Here are some examples of people who have done it.

Film Eight Ltd

John Stephens was a photographer, working for an advertising agency. A friend of his, Tom Briggs, worked for a television company. Tom specialised in processing film for large companies.

Together, they thought up a new idea: an easier and simpler way of processing cine film taken by amateurs on holiday, at weddings etc. They spent a lot of time messing about in a small workshop, experimenting with their process. They hadn't enough money to manufacture the process themselves, so the bank suggested that they should approach a local company which might be able to manufacture their product.

The two inventors made a prototype and took it along to a nearby factory. The managing director welcomed the idea and said he could cope with the problems of production. With Tom and John, he formed a completely new company, Film Eight Ltd, and began to make the new product. Using the bigger company's marketing knowledge and expertise, they made a success of the venture and Tom and John are now at work on their second idea.

SHOWING NOW, A RANGE OF BEAUTIFUL HAND FRAMED SWEATERS IN MOHAIR, WOOL ETC.

For details contact:—

June Hight

AND ARRANGE AN APPOINTMENT

* Bring this advert along and claim 10% discount
PRICES START AROUND £30

What's your idea?

Ask yourself – what could I do?

If you are still at school or at college maybe you won't have much to write. You are still in the learning stage. Even so, it's a useful plan to write down a list of your skills, your work experience (if you have any) and your ideas. This could lead to a business plan and an opportunity later on.

In your notebook, make out lists under these suggestions.
1 Things I enjoy doing.
2 Things I am good at.
3 Things I am not so good at.
4 Skills I can offer.
5 Hobbies and interests with business possibilities.
6 Work experience and jobs which I've had.

Then there's another essential list to be made. In business, you will always be learning, picking up new information and ideas. Let's start now with what you think you *need* to know.

List the skills and experience which you will need to go into business? Divide your list into:
- technical skills.
- business and managing skills.

If you didn't have much idea of how to answer the last question, here are some of the jobs you would have to do in order to make a business idea work.

> Make a list of people who could help you – friends, family, other business people.
> Talk to someone who has experience of this kind of work.
> List the skills you'll need.
> Plan the financial side of the business.
> Prepare a publicity plan – advertising, leaflets, press release.
> Carry out market research to find out what people really want.
> Work out costs, prices and the point when you'd make a profit.
> Learn the business skills to do all these tasks.
> Assess where you've got to after 3 months, 6 months, a year.
> Arrange distribution – transport, post.
> Plan how to raise the money to start up in business.

These points aren't in the right order. But every one is important.

Choose six of the steps which *you* would need to tackle in order to make your business idea work.

5
Research, product planning and development

Many companies have a special department called 'R & D'. This stands for *research and development*. In this department are the thinkers, the planners, the product designers – the 'Think Tank' of the company.

The job of R & D is to design products or services, or improve existing products, basing ideas on what the market researchers tell them about customers' needs and wants. Sometimes, of course, R & D comes up with a completely new idea which no one has thought of. The job of market research is then reversed. They have to go to work to find out what customers think of this idea – but at the same time they have to prevent rival companies from hearing about this marvellous new invention.

The specialists who work in R & D or the product planning department could be a mixture of designers and engineers. Take for example, a new microcomputer. The company (let's call it *Home Micros Ltd*) already sells micros. But they desperately need a 'new look' to recapture dwindling sales and to catch up on advancing technology.

The industrial designers, engineers and electronics wizards plan and build the new micro. Another group of researchers think about its appearance:
- it must have an easy-to-use keyboard.
- it must have colour.
- it must have some special technical feature which lifts it into a special category.

Another person will look at packaging design. Experts will be called in. How will the micro be boxed, labelled, made attractive to customers?

By this time, everyone is involved. The R & D section, which started it, will have drawn on the information provided by the market researchers, and will have consulted the sales and marketing people who have to sell the micro. They will have firm views about what will sell, and what won't sell. At each stage, too, the production department and finance people will be asked for their opinion. Can it be made at low cost? What will be the final cost, and the price in the shops? The R & D section cannot answer all the questions. But they have to know some answers. Otherwise they could design and make a beautiful new micro which costs £500 to make, when rival companies are selling much the same thing for £300. Result? The end of that R & D department or the company, if it goes ahead!

R & D in industry

The task of the R & D section then is:
- to design a product which customers want.
- to make sure it can be made at low cost so that it is at a price the customer will pay.

This may sound easy, but it is often very difficult. After all, it is *ideas* that come first. No business will survive for long if it doesn't have ideas that change the product to meet changing needs and fashions.

Sometimes, the R & D department is part of market research or the marketing and sales department. Sometimes it is a 'special team'

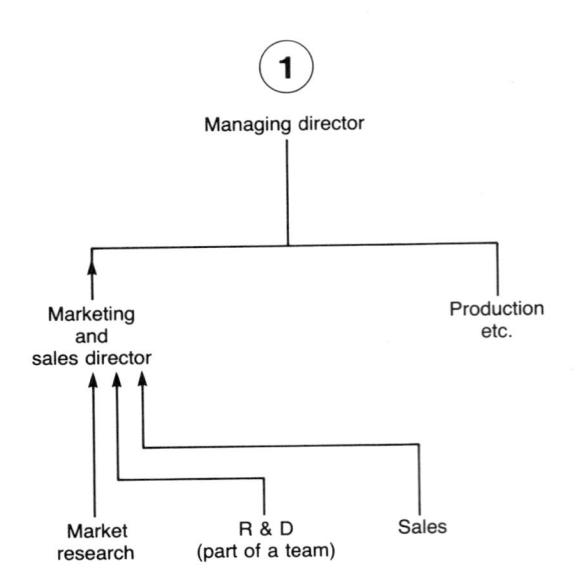

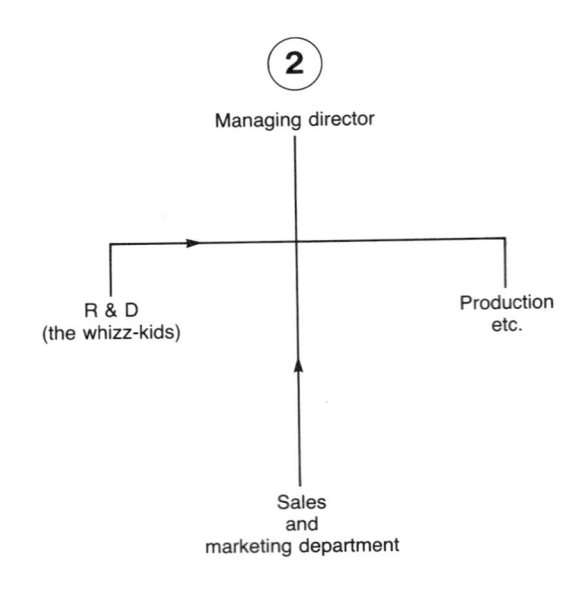

1

```
         Managing director
              |
    ┌─────────┴─────────┐
 Marketing           Production
   and                 etc.
sales director
    ↑↑↑
 ┌──┼──┐
Market  R & D   Sales
research (part of a team)
```

2

```
         Managing director
              |
    ┌─────────┼─────────┐
  R & D              Production
(the whizz-kids)       etc.
              |
           Sales
            and
      marketing department
```

under the direct control of the managing director, and acts as a team of 'whizz-kids' to develop new ideas. In the fast-moving world of computers and electronics, it is often the R & D section which *is the business*. There have been many examples of an engineer with an idea or a new development who has come out of the backroom of R & D to take over as technical director or who has left the company entirely, in order to start up his or her own new business.

Here are two diagrams to show how the R & D can fit into the organisation of a business. The R & D section is part of a large team. It is called the 'direct connection' model. Which method do you think the R & D people would prefer? Why?

Industrial design

One of the main reasons why industry keeps changing and developing is because of *design*.

The word design probably means something different to you. It could be a project in an art lesson such as drawing shapes and patterns. But think of furniture design, buildings, computers, cars — they all have to be designed, planned and made to work.

We are getting closer to the meaning of *industrial design*. This is concerned with what the product looks like, and how people can make the best use of it. Another kind of design is *engineering design* which concentrates on how mechanical and electrical things work, and how they perform under all kinds of stresses and strains.

Do you recognise the aeroplane in the picture? This was the product of a form of engineering design. It can travel faster than the speed of sound. It can cross the Atlantic from the USA to Britain in under 4 hours. It can fly at a speed of 1450 mph.

The designers of the Concorde had to face all kinds of complex technical problems. But they started with one factor — the aeroplane had to carry travellers on transatlantic and world flights, at a price which some people would pay.

The customers came first. The technical problems came afterwards. Both were solved. The remaining factor – price – was a lot harder to answer. Concorde was very expensive to build and its construction had to be helped by government money.

Industrial designers are concerned with all kinds of products, and with all stages of manufacture. You see the evidence of their work every day in fashion; in the interiors of shops; in offices and homes; in engineering and industry.

Make your own design

A good designer has to balance these factors:
- the object designed actually works – that is it *functions*.
- it is pleasing to the eye and satisfies the *customer*.
- it can be sold, which means there is a *market* for it at a *price* that people will be willing to pay.

Let's see if you can design something. Choose from one of these products. By means of drawings and plans, illustrate your design, and explain any special features it may have.
- a car
- an aeroplane
- a piece of furniture
- a fashion accessory
- some kind of packaging for food or cosmetics

6
Market research, or who'll buy what we're selling

Most businesses depend on the answer to a very important question which is 'Can we sell it?'. 'It' is the product or service. The buyers are people, customers, often called 'the general public', but usually special groups of the public – householders, children, business people, overseas visitors and so on.

The *Marketing* department tries to solve this question. The people who work in this department provide the first (1) the middle (2) and the last (3) link in the chain of a company's business plan. The reason is that the Marketing department has these tasks.

1 To find out what the customer wants before the product or service is designed, made and put on sale.
2 To prepare the customer for the arrival of the product while it is being made.
3 To sell and deliver the product to the customer.

In the next few chapters, we shall be looking at these tasks in more detail. Let's start with the first link in the chain – *market research*.

Market research

This is the name given to the job of finding out what people need or want, and whether they would pay for it. This can be carried out in various ways. One method is to ask people for opinion. This is how researchers find out how people are likely to vote in a forthcoming election. They will ask, say, 500 people in various parts of the country if they intend to vote Conservative, Labour, Liberal, SDP etc, and add up the results.

The same method can be used for a new product. Interviewers stop people in the street, or knock at doors, and ask questions about the type of product. For instance, if they are researching for a new kind of toothpaste, they would ask people about the taste of the toothpaste which they use at the moment; why they like it; its price; whether it's hard or easy to squeeze out of the tube; and so on.

There are advantages and disadvantages of this method of research.

Advantages
- direct contact with possible customers.
- the interviewer can make sure that questions are answered.
- if 500 replies is the target, the interviewers can keep going until 500 people have been asked.

Disadvantages
- it is expensive – paying interviewers, travelling to different parts of the country etc.
- it may be an unrepresentative sample (for instance, the toothpaste interviewers might pick on 100 people out of the 500 with false teeth.

Can you think of other advantages and disadvantages of such personal interviewing techniques?

Prototypes
Another way of testing the market is to make the product – a model or a prototype – and ask people to use it. This could be done for the toothpaste example – the sample of 500 people are given, free, a supply of toothpaste to use for a few weeks and their opinions are then tested by interview or questionnaire.

What are the advantages and disadvantages of this method?

Market knowledge
Companies which have been making much the same product for years, such as those in the engineering industries, already know a lot about their industry. The researchers would start here, going to the main customers who already buy their products, and asking them advice about a new idea.

Let's take the example of a new aeroplane engine. Rolls Royce, who already make engines for ten airlines around the world (USA, Japan, France, UK), wouldn't go out on to the streets with a questionnaire. They would concentrate on their ten customers, and discuss each stage of the aircraft engine design with them, making sure that the engines dovetailed into other aspects of new aeroplane design which these customers might be considering.

Questionnaires
This is a popular way of testing public opinion. A printed questionnaire is sent to customers, or a section of the public, asking for their opinion about a new product. For instance, a newspaper company recently proposed to publish a new monthly magazine on computing. They sent out 10 000 copies of a questionnaire, to be distributed through computer shops, asking people for their opinion on what might go into this magazine. Unfortunately, they received only 181 replies. What do you think went wrong with this market research idea?

Choose your choc bar
Let's suppose that a chocolate manufacturer is faced with the task of finding out what customers think of a new chocolate bar. Instead of a 'wild sample' (that is, anyone at all) the market researchers would try to seek out chocolate-bar eaters who would give a more accurate sample of opinions.

To choose this group, they would consider three *market factors*:
- *age*: 60 per cent of chocolate-bar eaters are known to be in the age range of 8 to 21.
- *income*: the bar would cost 20p – who would be able to buy at that price? Would it be mostly teenagers?
- *sex*: Would girls or boys, Mums or Dads, grandmas or grandads be more likely to buy?

The manufacturer, whose market researchers might be using questionnaires, personal interviewing or prototypes (free choc bars) should target inquiries at a selected sample of 500 people.

Which age-group and income-group is most likely to buy the bars?

Here are three products. How would you select a sample 500 people if you were set the task of finding out people's opinions of these three products?

1 a pram
2 cat-food
3 jeans

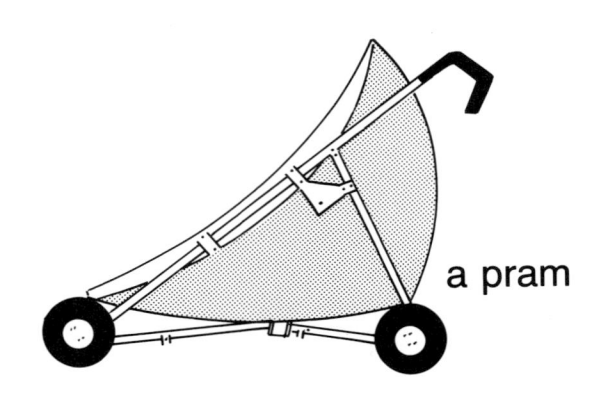

a pram

choc bar with others. But they may not know the price of choc bars, and say something silly, such as '2p', or '50p'.

It gets worse. Having asked 500 people if they like the bar and would buy it, there is no guarantee that when the bars are made and are in the shops, that the 500 are going to rush there to buy them! Market research is a hazardous business, as you can see, for if the researchers are wrong, and recommend making and selling something which is ignored by customers, the company will be left with a product which it cannot sell and will lose a great deal of money.

Plan your own research

Think of a new product or service or choose from these:
- a new line in sweaters
- a new microcomputer
- a local baby-minding service

In your notebook, draw up the plan for your market research. Use various techniques such as door-to-door inquiries, questionnaires, sampling, local knowledge and any other methods you can think of.

MARKET RESEARCH PLAN

PRODUCT ....

NUMBER OF PEOPLE TO BE INTERVIEWED	METHODS	SELECTION by		
		AGE	INCOME	SEX

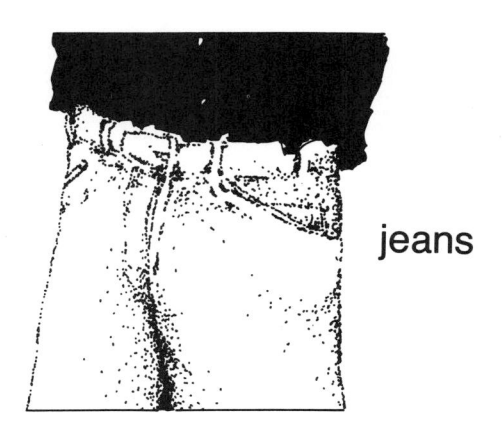

Questions, questions . . .

Another difficulty in market research is in framing questions. If you ask people the obvious question 'Would you buy this choc bar?', they are very likely to say 'yes'. If you then asked, 'How much would you pay for it?', you'd be asking them to *think*. They could compare this

jeans

Expanding the firm

7
Pricing, or can you make a profit?

Let's suppose you are a manager in a manufacturing company which makes and sells kitchen equipment such as coffee machines, electric kettles, toasters, mixers and so on. An idea has been born in the research lab. It's a revolutionary machine, a combination of toaster, sandwich-maker and tea-brewer. It can turn two slices of bread and a filling of e.g. meat, cheese, tomato into a toasted sandwich, while making a brew of tea, using teabags and dried milk.

The idea is passed to the engineers in the research workshop who make a prototype.

The market research department now move in. They have already been consulted, in the early stages of the project, on whether it is a product which is likely to sell. Now they move to the second stage, to test customer reaction. The marketing people have also come up with the brand-name – the 'Toaster Tea Box'.

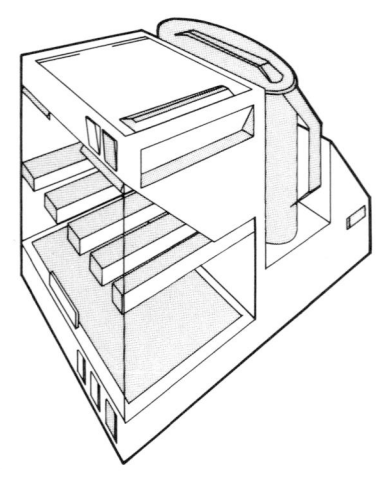

The Toaster Tea Box

Photographs and copies of the prototype are shown to 200 potential customers. When they are asked 'Would you buy this?', most people reply, 'Well, I might, but how much is it?' The marketing department had, of course, been expecting this question. They had already decided on a likely price of about £22, based on estimates of manufacturing and other costs.

The first feedback from the prototype research was favourable. Now came decision-time. **1** Should the Toaster Tea Box be put into production? **2** How many should be made? **3** What should be the actual price?

Decision **1** is made – to manufacture 10 000 Toaster Tea Boxes in the first year. The factory swings into action. The marketing department begins planning the sales compaign. While this is going on, the managers are working out the *price*. To do this, they need to do some arithmetic!

Fixed costs and variable costs

The first stage in finding a price is to add up the *costs*. For example, to make 10 000 Toaster Tea Boxes, the company would need:
- to rent or buy a factory.
- to provide offices, telephones, staff.
- to pay the wages of the factory workers.
- to buy or hire machinery and machine tools.
- to buy the raw materials – steel, glass, plastic, or whatever is needed to make the product.

Some of these costs are already known. The company already has a factory. It has offices, and machinery which can be adapted. So the outlay is not as tremendous as you might think.

On the other hand, these oncoming business expenses, usually called *fixed costs* or *overheads*, have to be met. This is done by adding the costs, or a part of them, to the bill for making the 10 000 Toaster Tea Boxes.

Then there are the *variable costs* (sometimes called *direct costs*). These depend on the number of TTBs to be made. It will obviously cost more to produce 10 000 than 5000. Variable costs include raw materials, wages, advertising, transport, postage and so on — that is everything involved in getting the TTBs directly to the customer.

To find the price, we have to add these costs together and divide by the number of TTBs. Let's assume the proportion of fixed costs which have to be carried by this new product is £60 000 a year. To this should be added the variable costs. It has been found that it costs £8 to make one TTB. The true cost of making 10 000 is therefore:

£8 × 10 000 = £80 000
plus fixed costs of £60 000
total £140 000

So, it costs £140 000 to make 10 000 TTBs. One TTB therefore costs **£14** to make, if the fixed costs are added.

But if *more* TTBs were manufactured, the *unit price* (the price of one) would drop. Look at this sum for making 15 000 TTBs:

£8 × 15 000 = £120 000
plus fixed costs £60 000
total £180 000

Divide the total cost (£180 000) by 15 000 TTBs, and the unit cost is now **£12**.

Why do you think the cost per article is less if more are produced?

Suppose the TTBs were a great success, and it was decided to manufacture 20 000 in the second year. What would be the unit cost then?

Cost-plus-profit pricing

So far, then, we have arrived at a unit cost of £14 for 10 000 Toaster Tea Boxes. What about the profit? What should the company aim for? They think that a price of around £24 to £28 is critical. What will the customer pay? The managers know that if the TTBs are priced at £24, they will sell more than if the price is £28. But what if they could make more profit by selling less TTBs but make more money on each one? They decide on this second alternative, that is to set the price at around the £28 mark (double the £14 cost price). But this £14 isn't total profit. There are likely to be other costs that haven't yet been added and of course, tax will have to be paid on any eventual profit.

We have been discussing here a pricing policy which is called 'cost-plus-profit pricing'. Many goods in the shops are priced in this way.

You have to remember that the 'price' here is the shop price. The manufacturer may have to give the retailer (the shops) a hefty *discount*. For instance, if the shop price (that is, how much Ms Smith pays) is £25, then the retailer may buy at £20, taking *his/her* profit of £5 on each sale. The manufacturer has therefore already lost £5 of the £25 price, and knowing this, the manufacturer might decide, right at the start, that the shop price must be £30.

Now you can see why a price in a shop is a great deal more than the manufacturing cost (which was £8 for each Toaster Tea Box!).

Market price

Another way of pricing a product is to look carefully at what the competitors are asking. For example, our manufacturer already makes coffee machines. But there are about six main kinds of coffee-maker in the shops. All are around the same price, £28. If a manufacturer decides to price a new coffee-maker at £30, there has to be a special reason to do so, such as more cups per brew, or a similar attraction. Otherwise, sales will be low.

The makers of the Toaster Tea Box know this. But at the moment there isn't a rival in the shops, so they can ask £30 and get away with it. In the end, they decide on £29.50 — it doesn't sound quite as much as £30! The next manufacturer to get into this business will look at this price and mark their new TTB at, say, £27.50. Or the newcomers might decide to go for £32.50, hoping that the customer will think the new TTB is a much better one, making the higher price worthwhile.

The 'break-even' point of sales

We know that it costs £140 000 to make 10 000 TTBs (£14 unit price x 10 000).

At some point along the road, the company reaches the *break-even* point. This is when a sufficient number of articles (TTBs in our case) is sold to pay the total costs. After this magic number has been reached, every TTB from then on is *profitable.*

If sales fall below the target, then the

company makes a *loss*, not a profit. If the price of each TTB is £30, work out in your notebook how many have to be sold to reach the break-even point?

Making it pay

The Toaster Tea Box was a manufacturing idea, something which a big company might go in for. But pricing is just as important for small businesses. In fact, it is *more* important, because a large company can cushion a mistake or absorb a trading loss, if they have other products which are selling well. But a small company is at risk if a mistake is made. So 'the price must be right' has to be the slogan! Let's look at a real example.

A group of trainees on a MSC scheme decided to make children's toys, children's clothes and cushions from scraps of material they obtained free from factory with surplus stock.

The direct costs and fixed costs were small. They had the local Youth Club as the 'factory'. Two fathers said they could use their garages as warehouses. They had to buy some extra materials, and they hired sewing machines.

One of the first tasks of the trainees (they called themselves 'The Rag Traders') was to fix on a unit cost. They added together the cost of all materials they had to buy – threads, buttons, padding. Their speciality was a padded dog and a grinning teddy bear. The production cost of one toy came to 20p, assuming they made and sold 100 of each. This included rental on the machines, electricity and a contribution (not much) to the Youth Club funds. Transport cost nothing: they offered to deliver toys, cushions and anything else within a ten-mile radius of the Youth Club – by bike!

Labour costs

The Rag Traders had, so far, added nothing for labour. They were on an MSC scheme and had trainee allowances, so they didn't have to earn a wage. But to put the whole thing on to a proper commercial basis, they added 30p as a labour cost. Total costing is now 50p – this is sometimes called the *job cost* for it has absorbed everything – overheads, variable costs and labour.

They also decided again on a commercial rate for profit. The price of the teddies and dogs was fixed at £1. This was a 50 per cent increase over the job cost. How much profit were they planning to make on each article?

In pricing policies, there are several important things to remember.

- There are likely to be extra costs which may not have been thought of. If the price is too low, the profit will be lost in paying these extras.
- Look for *at least* a 50 per cent return – the real profit will be a lot less than this.
- Some costs will rise. Among them are labour costs, the purchase of materials, petrol etc.
- The Rag Traders have had a 'cushioned' start! If they were really in business independent of the Youth Club and their helpful parents, there would be extra costs such as workshop, warehouse and labour. The 'uncushioned' price of a teddy bear would be around £2.

Try it

Think of something you could sell. If you haven't got an idea, assume you have the means of production and the skill to make something. Work out the likely costs – the fixed costs and the variable costs. Think of a reasonable price at which you could sell your product. Work out your income. What profits would you expect to make?

8
Going after the money

Most people who start up in business need money. It may only be £100 to buy ladders and paint, but to raise that amount can be as difficult for a beginner as it is for a large company to raise £1 million.

What's the money for?

Here are some of the reasons why money might be needed to start up a business.
- to pay for equipment, tools, machinery.
- to buy raw materials or components.
- to pay wages.
- for advertising, postage, stationery etc.

Make a list of *other* reasons which you can think of?

All of these needs can be put into two groups. For new businesses *start-up capital* is needed. The money needed for buildings and machinery is usually called *fixed capital*. Then, once the business has been established, there's the money that's needed to buy materials, pay staff and so on. This is usually called *operating* or *circulating capital*.

Where does the money come from?

It is possible that the family will help. This could be in the form of a loan, or by buying shares (if it is a limited company). Friends, too, might contribute. But if you were to start up in business for yourself, you would be expected to put in most of the capital, or go hunting for it.

The bank

The first call you might make could be to the bank. Banks are not all that keen to lend money. They have to be persuaded. After all, they are taking a risk, and banks aren't noted as big risk-takers, at least with people who walk in off the street!

On the other hand, banks want to help people to start up in business, or make a small one into a very large and profitable business so that they too can make money. So they are always willing to be approached. But it's no good going along to the bank and saying, 'Could I have £2000, please!'.

Making a case: the mini-skip

No matter if the application to a bank is for a small or large amount of money, much the same procedure applies – a 'case' has to be made by the applicant. Let's take an example.

Alex Hodgson worked for an engineering company. He saw that there was a need for a mini-skip, smaller than the huge ones used on building sites to dump rubbish, earth, stones. His idea was to make a skip that could be pulled by an ordinary car or van. It seemed to Alex that the market for a small skip like this could be very large indeed and would include all those householders doing gardening or repairs who needed a vehicle to take rubbish to the Council tip.

Alex set to work at home and designed his skip. He added up all his savings which came to £5000. He sold a lump of his large garden to a house-builder for another £10 000. A friend agreed to put in £5000. Total raised: £20 000. But, to get started, he needed at least another £20 000. Before he went to the bank he set out his 'business plan'.

Business plan
Aim
To manufacture and sell 20 skips in the first year, increasing to 60 in the second, and 100 in the third year.

Market
- Eight building companies, with known managers, who have already said they are willing to consider purchasing one.
- Other building and engineering contractors: about 300 companies known throughout the UK.
- Other building companies and do-it-yourself suppliers: 80 companies or contacts known.
- Home market, reached by direct sales through advertisements in newspapers and magazines, or by selling through DIY suppliers.

Production
- a small rented factory with office, obtained from local authority under a Government scheme to assist small businesses: rental is £600 a year.
- purchase of equipment and components
  1st year – £10 000
  2nd year – £22 000
  3rd year – £40 000
- wages
  1st year – £10 000
  2nd year – £15 000
  3rd year – £30 000
- manufacturing
  1st year – £10 000
  2nd year – £12 000
  3rd year – £16 000
- extra or additional costs: telephone, stationery, furniture, transport, etc.
  1st year – £600
  2nd year – £800
  3rd year – £1000

Total costs for first three years (£)

	1st year	2nd year	3rd year
Rent	600	600	600
Materials	10 000	22 000	40 000
Wages	10 000	15 000	30 000
Manufacturing	10 000	12 000	16 000
Extras	600	800	1 000
Totals:	31 200	50 400	87 600

Other costs
This isn't the whole story. Alex will find that there are other *costs*. Think about them.

What other costs can you think of? Make a list.

What *weaknesses* can you see in this business? Make a list of what you think might be dangers and weaknesses.

The interview
When Alex sat down with the bank manager, the interview went something like this:

Alex: In the letter and papers I sent you earlier, I explained my business plan and how I needed £20 000 to get started.

Manager: Well, of course, the bank has to be careful, Mr Hodgson. Although you have been a successful engineer, you haven't *managed* a business before.

Alex: No, that's why I'm here, that is to get started.

Manager: I see you are putting your own money into it. Can't you raise any more?

Alex: I've raised £15 000 myself. And a friend, who incidentally is a businessman, and a successful one, is prepared to back me with £5000. We've worked out that we need to double that amount of money, but we can't raise any more ourselves.

Manager: Hmm, and when do you expect to break-even?

Alex: If we sell 20 skips in the first year, at a price of around £2000 each, that should be enough to pay for materials for the second year. We've calculated that we'll be into profits by the end of the third year, assuming we sell the full

number of skips. If sales are really good, we could be into profit by the end of the second year.
Manager: Well, perhaps. Anyway, there are two possible ways of helping you. One is by a *bank loan*. We would lend you, say £20 000, over three or five years. You would of course have to pay annual interest, and the rate of interest is around 16 per cent at present. The interest would have to be added to your list of outgoings for those three years, of course.
Alex: Crumbs!
Manager: Well, Mr Hodgson, no one is going to lend you money for nothing. Anyway, the second method is to let you run up a *bank overdraft*. You could draw money from the bank, going up to, say, a limit of £5000 overdraft a month. You would have to pay much the same interest – 16 per cent – but it works out cheaper than a full loan, because you only borrow as you need it. The drawback is that *you can't use this money as fixed capital*: you will have to find that yourself. You can use the overdraft money only as operating capital.
Alex: I'll have to go away and work out the costs of borrowing.
Manager: Yes, you will. And we'd need some kind of guarantee. Do you have an insurance policy or mortgage you could offer as a guarantee, Mr Hodgson?

Venture capital

As you can see, the bank manager isn't making it easy for Alex. His experience is shared by many other starters. Banks are much more willing to lend to well-established companies who have proved their success already.

There are other ways of raising money. One is through *venture capital* companies. These are organisations with money to lend. But they are just as difficult to convince as banks. Venture capital companies are led by accountants and financiers: they will invest money in a new venture but only after they have explored its chances of success. To do this, they will look closely at the product (Alex's skip), look at the market for it (building, engineering and DIY companies and the general public), and then work out over, say, three years, what the return on the investment will be.

If the answers look good, they might offer to invest £20 000, but again at a high rate of interest.

Government financial help

Instead of going to a bank or a venture capital company, Alex Hodgson could have looked around for a government grant.

The Department of Trade and Industry helps people through the *Small Firms Service*. It offers free advice on business matters, including how to find low-interest loans. If you are interested and want to find out more, write to the SFS, 123 Victoria Street, London SW1E 6RV. In addition, there are 12 Small Firms centres around Britain: they can be contacted by ringing Freephone 2444.

The Manpower Services Commission (MSC), another government department, runs the *Enterprise Allowance Scheme*. People who are self-employed and who have £1000 or more a year to invest in setting up their own business can get up to £40 a week income for a year, to tide them over. Alex Hodgson could have benefited from this scheme.

In 1983, the Government began a new programme called the *Business Expansion Scheme* by which big companies, assisted by the Government, provide money for investment.

However, all of these schemes involved a lot of paperwork, and to get the best advantage from them, a small business or individual might have to employ an accountant or solicitor.

Local authorities

In order to attract industry to their areas, some local authorities can offer very attractive incentives. For instance, government allowances can be claimed by companies setting up business in *Enterprise Zones*. Local councils can also offer low rents for factories, or even allow a company or new business to have offices rent-free for a year or two.

There are lots of other ways by which government departments and local councils can help business. The ways in which they can help can be summarised as:
- rent and rate rebates.
- offices, workshops or factories at low rents.
- business start-up money (but at high interest rates).
- tax allowances for smaller companies.

Questions

Make a list of the various ways of financing a business. Start with borrowed money, then go on to government aid schemes.

9
'Shall we go public?'

Expanding the firm

The ways by which a small company can be set up and financed have been described. At some stage, the directors may consider that the time has come to 'go public'. Let's look at the stages in this process.

'Super Screens Ltd' is a small company which began by writing and manufacturing software for computer systems. The firm expanded, and started to make its own desk-top micros.

The demand for goods – both software and micros – was constant. Overseas sales have been very encouraging, and there are signs that a big order from the USA is possible. In the R & D section, the 'boffins' think they have discovered an electronic breakthrough which would reduce the size of a desk-top computer. The sales department say they could do much better if they had another twelve sales reps and regional offices in other parts of the country.

There are *advantages* in expanding Super Screens Ltd. What are they?

There are *disadvantages* and dangers, too.

One is that the expansion of the sales force and the building of a new factory to cope with the demand for more micros and software means that there must be a big investment of money. Where is it to come from? And, supposing the company does all this, and builds a new factory, there are other expenses ahead – extra staffing costs; money needed to furnish and equip offices, workshops and the factory; transport costs . . . and so on. Another danger is the business itself. There's a lot of competition in the computer business. What if sales don't increase? What if a competitor brings out a new computer, half the size but twice the memory capacity of Super Screens' new product? All these are dangers.

Suppose you are a director of Super Screens Ltd. Make a list of the advantages and disadvantages of expansion. Then, looking at the two sets of ideas and information, decide what you would do.

Finding the money

The decision has been taken by the Board of Super Screens Ltd. They have decided to expand. They estimate that the financial investment needed is £500 000.

There are various ways of finding the money. One is to go to their bankers and ask for a loan or an overdraft. If they did this, the total control of the company would remain with the directors. On the other hand, they are taking on a huge debt, and the interest charges alone would be crippling.

Another way of raising the money is to 'go public'. This means transferring the private company into a public company by selling shares on the Stock Exchange. The directors of Super Screens Ltd decide to take this path.

The Stock Exchange

The Stock Exchange is an indoor marketplace. It's a place where private companies and the Government can raise money to finance new activities. This is done by the issue of stocks and shares.

There are branches and brokers' offices in several UK cities. The most important branch is in London, where there has been a Stock Exchange since the 17th century.

In March 1986, there were around 4300 *members* of the Stock Exchange in about 230 firms. To be elected, a person has to have been

The trading floor of the London Stock Exchange

with a member firm for three years and pass a qualifying exam. Some firms have up to 40 partners and 500 support staff cover their research, advisory and investment services. But there are small firms, too, with just two partners.

The Stock Exchange is currently undergoing radical changes to institute a new dealing system based on competing 'market makers.' This will bring it into line with stock exchanges in the rest of the world. In the old system, members were either jobbers or stockbrokers (often simply called 'brokers'). Between them they controlled all buying and selling of shares for, unlike a marketplace, the general public cannot buy and sell direct to each other.

Jobbers, experts in their knowledge of companies and the ups and downs of the stock market, worked on the floor of the Stock Exchange, buying and selling shares. They dealt only with the brokers.

Brokers dealt with clients, customers and companies wanting to buy and sell stocks and shares, or who want financial advice on all kinds of subjects. In the new 'broker-dealers' system, there will be two types of agents: those who continue to act just as brokers, obtaining for their clients the best price from the 'market makers;' and those who act as both broker and dealer. The latter will belong to firms known as *market makers* and will specialise in a particular section of the market, e.g. finance.

Brokers took a fixed commission or fee – usually 1¼ per cent – on the business they transacted for a client. For instance, if a stockbroker bought £5000 worth of shares for a client, the fee would be £62.50. On 31 October 1986, the fixed-commission system will be abolished and a system of *negotiated* commissions will be introduced. This will mean that people wishing to buy or sell stocks or shares will be able to 'shop around' for the most favourable commission rate. This will make the whole system far more competitive.

The Financial Services Bill, which will clearly define the roles of people like jobbers and broker, and spell out in detail how the new system will operate and be regulated, is expected to be published in late 1986.

Each day, business totalling several hundreds of million pounds is transacted on the Stock Exchange. To cope with the vast volume of paperwork, about 15 000 people are employed, either in the Exchange or by member firms.

Kinds of shares

Stocks fall into two main categories – *fixed interest* and *equities*.

With fixed interest stocks, the amount that is received in interest is known in advance. For instance, if you bought £100 worth of 7½% Treasury Stock, you would get £7.50 interest each year for every £100 held. One group of stock is called *Gilts*. This is fixed interest Government stock (gilt-edged in its guarantees). Gilts are said to be the most secure stock to possess because the Government stands behind them.

Other fixed interest stocks are *local government loans*, which are also guaranteed, often for a period of, say, ten years. This means that a percentage interest is paid each year for ten years.

A *debenture* is another stock in this category. It is a loan and is backed by a legal agreement, rather like a mortgage, of repayment in a certain amount of years.

Preference shares come between debentures and equities. They also carry a fixed rate of dividend but this need not be paid out by the directors if a company's profits are too low to justify the payout.

Equities are shares where nothing is fixed. The directors meet each year to recommend a dividend which depends on the profits made in that year. The shares are called equities because the holders share in the 'equity' of the company, that is they part-own it. These shares carry the biggest risk but also the best prospects of future growth and therefore profit. Ordinary shareholders have the right to speak and vote at general meetings of the company.

Dividends

When people buy shares issued by a public company, they naturally expect to share in its success. Shareholders are entitled to part of the profits which are distributed by the company. This is the *dividend*.

However, if a company hasn't done well and there is no profit, the directors can decide not to pay a dividend. The danger then is that the shareholders will lose confidence in the company and will sell their shares, thus pushing the market price of the company's shares downwards to, say, 70p for a £1 share.

Launching into public ownership

Let's now go back to Super Screens Ltd. The directors, needing £500 000, have decided to go public. They need someone to act for them, that is to deal with the financial details and negotiate on the Stock Exchange.

The directors therefore appoint a *sponsor*. This is usually a firm of stockbrokers or a merchant bank. In the case of Super Screens Ltd, they appoint one sponsor, a merchant bank which advises on all their investments and financial matters, and has arranged loans to the company previously.

The sponsors move into action. The business of Super Screens Ltd is closely analysed to see if they have got their sums right as to how much needs to be borrowed, and to plan the *prospectus*. This document is published: it contains information about Super Screens – its sales record; expected sales forecast for about three years ahead; its assets and liabilities; the names of the directors; its business prospects.

The Council of the Stock Exchange checks the accuracy of the prospectus. The Council's duty is to make sure that a company going public is a fair and honest one, for the general public are now to be invited to invest in it, and the Stock Exchange is determined that no 'dodgy' companies will be listed there.

The Council decides – Super Screens Ltd is a worthy company. A date is set for the sales to be available to the public. At this stage, Super Screens is said to have been 'granted a quotation'.

Advertisements are now placed in national newspapers, tempting people to buy shares. It has been decided to offer 500 000 shares at £1 each. By completing an application form and sending it to the sponsors, people can buy shares.

The sponsors have done a very good job. Within four days, all 500 000 shares are sold, and buying and selling begins on the floor of the Stock Exchange. Within another week, Super Screens' shares are at £1.25 per share. This means that if someone bought 1000 shares at £1 on the first day and sells them again two weeks later, a nice profit would be made. What is the profit?

The £500 000 received from the sale of shares, less the fee or commission paid to the sponsors, goes to Super Screens Ltd, who can now start building a factory and taking on more staff.

Test your knowledge

Have you understood all this? Test yourself by matching the words in A with the phrases in B. Write your answers in your notebook.

A	B
Debenture	Payment from a company's profits to shareholders.
Dividend	A fixed interest stock repayable within a time limit.
Equity	The risk-sharing part of a company's capital.
Gilts	A statement of the company's past record and future prospects.
Prospectus	Stock whose interest and capital is guaranteed by the Government.
Sponsor	A merchant bank or broker who prepares the prospectus.

10
Case-studies

Here are three case-studies of people who set up in business for different reasons and with different financial problems.. Read the case-studies, and then answer the questions about them.

'We thought we could do better . . .'

Bill Wright worked for 7 years as a cleaner in the offices of a shipping company. Then came the bombshell. He and his mate, George Adams, were made redundant. But within a week they had put in a bid for the cleaning contract . . . and they won it!

'George and I thought we could do the job better, anyway. But it took some nerve to offer to do the same job at our price. We were helped by our redundancy money, a golden handshake. We were tempted to live on it for a year, just do nothing. But we both knew that if we lazed around, we'd find it very hard to start work again.

'We both knew it was on the cards that we'd be paid off. The cleaning company we worked for were losing contracts right and left because the cleaners they employed didn't stay long — the wages weren't good — and the office owners were always complaining about things being left. Over a pint in the pub we'd talked about putting in a bid ourselves, but it was just a laugh until we got our redundancy money.

'We'd both been brought up in Hull and could look after ourselves when things got rough. I've had to stand on my feet and fight for what I want. In fact, George and I had even thought of packing in our jobs if we could win a cleaning contract.

'Well, it worked out like this. We went to the office manager of the shipping firm and asked if we had a chance. He knew we were reliable and good workers. His mouth fell open when we said, 'What about it, Mr Jackson, we'll take over from your contractors.'

'He said, "Put in a bid and see what happens." Right. Knowing what the other mob were paid for the cleaning work helped, of course, for we made sure our bid was a good bit lower. Our letter went in two days after we'd held a farewell party at our old company. A week later we were back at the shipping offices. This time we were the bosses. In the early days there were only two workers — George and me. Then we took on more staff. It was a bit nerve-wracking. We'd never been our own bosses. We'd never done the paperwork of running a business.

'But it didn't seem to matter. The bank showed us how to set up 'the books', the income and expenditure accounts for the business. We bought old vans, used (but not clapped out) equipment. We used our homes as offices until we could afford to hire a daytime office.

'But one contract wasn't enough. Within a month we'd put in three more bids and won two of them. Work began to come in. Now six companies use us. We employ eight part-time cleaners. And we are all busy.'

The business of finding nannies

Would you trust a 19-year-old girl to find a nanny to help you look after your children? Almost certainly, if it was Sarah Hiscock. She is a remarkable teenager (she's 20 in June), who since November has been running Dial A Nanny from a tiny front room in her family home in Southampton. Since she began, she has registered 70 nannies and 50 employers, and completed 36 placements.

Her aim is to provide child care, full- or part-time, to ordinary mothers juggling with the demands of job and home, who need time to themselves or emergency help for a small price. 'It's not for the idle rich,' she says firmly, 'but for mothers who want to shop without a tired child in tow, house hunt or return to work.' She aims to keep her fees low, charging employers £3.25 for registration, £2.25 for a list of suitable nannies and a top £12.35 (including VAT) if they appoint a full-time nanny over 30 hours a week. 'No other agency can compete,' she says. 'They charge up to £150 for introductions — one near here charges £50, which is obviously aiming at a certain sort of person.' In fact, she has now realised that her charges are too low and that she is not actually making money yet.

Sarah interviews prospective nannies, asks for two references and continues to keep in contact after placement. The first 70 who registered include 13 who are fully trained and experienced; 17 with the NNEB qualification; 25 with relevant experience (such as running playgroups) and 10 mothers with grown-up children. Age limits are 17 to 60. 'Lots are prepared to work for £1 an hour and just treat it like a hobby. Those with qualifications are usually more interested in money and ask £1.50 or £2 an hour,' she says.

Nannies and employers together decide on payment without involving Sarah. Mothers have included a solicitor going to the United States with her husband on a three-week squash tour ('granny could not manage alone'), a gaming inspector who works at night, nurses, a barmaid, a film producer, as well as women without paid jobs. Two-thirds of the mothers, though, work full- or part-time.

'After school,' Sarah recalls, 'I took a two-year preliminary residential child care course, which offers more scope than the Nursery Nurse Examination Board (NNEB) syllabus.' In the holidays she looked after babies.

On leaving college she decided to be a full-time nanny with a family nearby. 'The 10-month-old girl was getting too attached and called me Mummy. I thought there must be lots of mothers who wanted nannies for a few hours a week, and so I placed ads in shop windows. Soon I was working with seven families who between them had 14 children aged from three months to 11 years. On Saturdays I had five children from 7 am to 7 pm — I took them swimming and to the New Forest while their parents ran a market stall. Lots of people asked me to work and the times started clashing. And girls asked me how to get into child care.'

So she decided to open her agency. It took three months to set up.

'Last August I asked the advice of the Small Firms Service. I paid £108 for a licence to trade. I had to name my mother (who teaches the educationally subnormal) as my partner because licences are not usually given to you if you are under 21.' Planning permission to use a room in her house as an office cost £50. She spent £50 to hire an accountant for the first year — 'but I hope to do my own books in future. I've taken a business evening course. That cost £30. The answering machine was £150; the telephone £20; and the desk, chair and typewriter came to £65.' All in all, it cost her about £500 to set herself up.

She still works two days a week for regular customers.

Looking ahead . . .

'I try to live on that income,' Sarah says. 'Everyone tells me it will take me three years to break even.' But she is not worried about failing. She accepts that her fees will have to rise next year, if she is not to make a loss, but her main aim is to meet a need rather than to make a lot of money.

She is full of bright ideas for building on what she has already done. She has hired a large hall in Southampton on May Day, and she wants parents to bring outgrown clothes for a straight no-money swop and children to do the same with story books and comics. She has roped in one friend who is going into the frozen home-cooking business and another who draws portraits. Sarah plans to fly Dial a Nanny balloons and stage a fancy dress procession in the city centre. Later, she wants to arrange pub meetings and coffee mornings for nannies and a mid-summer picnic. She sees Dial a Nanny as part of a community network, a safety net for families, with precious little bureaucracy but lots of fun for children.

She is writing a leaflet about how to become a nanny, launching herself as a consultant on setting up similar agencies ('I've been giving tips away free in the past') and applying to become a limited company. Eventually, she wants to start a Dial A Nanny franchise.

. . . and looking back

Did it work? Some time later Sarah was asked how things were going.

'Well,' she replied. 'I've been running the business for over a year and so far it's been a great success. I've made over 60 introductions, and I have over 80 nannies registered with the agency.'

Sarah has also been asked to give lectures on nursing as a career to students at a local college, and she set up a stand at a local careers convention.

'Are you still working from your front room?' she was asked.

'Yes. But I'm hoping to find office premises soon. Perhaps I'll share with someone — to keep down the costs. I'm getting enquiries from all over Britain from people who want to follow the same line. I'd like to set up a service in every major city but that'll take time and will need a lot of expert advice.'

With so many enquiries, Sarah has written an information sheet about her business, and another on *Nannying as a Career*.

'Another idea I have is to produce a magazine for nannies and for families with articles about child care, places for lonely nannies to go to, and suitable places to take their children, as well as crosswords, competitions and lots more. Anyone interested in publishing it?'

Going it alone

Frankie James and Alison Kimble were with a building company. They had good jobs. Frankie was a technician, and Alison worked in the offices as a clerk in accounts.

They could have been there for years, except . . .

'Rumours were flying around, and then one day the Manager called a meeting in the canteen. The firm had gone bust and were all to be paid off within a week.'

It was a blow. What were they — and 60 other people — to do?

Frankie takes up the story.

'In my spare time, I made beer at home. People laughed at me, but they also drank it. Anyway, after two weeks on the dole, I started to sell the beer. Then I thought — why not sell kits instead of beer?

'My wife and Alison were friends. We decided to join up and went to the bank. The manager there was polite but that was about all. He said we needed something called "a business plan". Alison who knew about income and expenditure and other mysteries, said it wasn't a difficult job.

'We therefore planned it out. We needed £8000 to get going. By using redundancy money and borrowing from family and friends, we got to £5000. We drew up a statement showing what we'd spend over the next year, and where the money (income) was to come from. Then back to see the manager of the bank. "Alright" he said, "I'll lend you £5000." The interest charges were fierce, but never mind, it got us going.

'At home, I'd already made some kits — 30 of them. While Alison and my wife made more kits, I tramped around shops, trying to sell the 30. Amazingly, I sold them in two weeks. Back home, we went into production. We made and sold 200 kits in three months. Within a year, we'd rented a 1500 square-foot factory from the Council (at a low rent), and were in production, manufacturing home-brew beer kits.

'Alison, Janet (that's my wife) and I are far happier. We're self-employed. We are our own bosses. We're also going grey (and we're young!). There's a lot of worry. But at the end of the day you know that all the effort you've made is for your own benefit and not the Big Boy Building Company, or whoever.

'I do the selling: that means for 5 days a week I'm out on the road. Alison looks after the factory, where we employ six people. I'm taking on a second salesman next month. The family are happy too. They all saw how the stress of starting up, borrowing and taking on factory space was worrying me, but they supported us.

'We've just had our first orders from Ireland (they seem to like beer there), Canada and Malta. I'm looking to the day when exports are 20 to 30 per cent of the business. At the moment they are only 5 per cent.

'I'd recommend people "to go it alone." But you've got to be careful. You must have a business idea that'll work. The most difficult thing in the world is to find a project that'll make money. Everyone's trying to think of one but few succeed. But why don't you put your brains to work and think up a brilliant idea. You might make your first million before I do.'

Answer these questions

Bill and George

1 What kind of work did they do before being made redundant?
2 Why were they successful in winning the contract? Make a list of the reasons for their success.
3 What materials, equipment and vehicles did they need? What else do you think they would need for the contract job? Make a list.

Sarah

1 What is the name of Sarah's business? Is it a good title?
2 What *is* Sarah's business?
3 What kind of training did she have?
4 She spent up to £500 to get going. What was the money spent on?
5 Which of Sarah's other ideas do you think might be successful?

Frankie and Alison

1 What is their business? Explain it in your own words.
2 What advantages did they have to start with?
3 What's a business plan? Explain it in your own words.
4 How much money did they raise themselves? How much did they borrow from the bank? What does 'the interest charges were fierce' mean?
5 Make a list of the reasons why you think Alison and Frankie have been successful.
6 What are the advantages and the disadvantages of being self-employed?

Industry and commerce

11
The location of industry

The production process

Much of the work of industry is based on a sequence of converting *raw materials* into *finished products*. In between, there are likely to be several production processes. They will involve design, planning, plant (machines), the employment of skilled labour, the use of power (energy), money, and distribution of products to customers.

The process can be shown like this:

Raw materials → Design and planning → Plant → Production processes (skilled labour, finance, power) → Finished products → Distribution

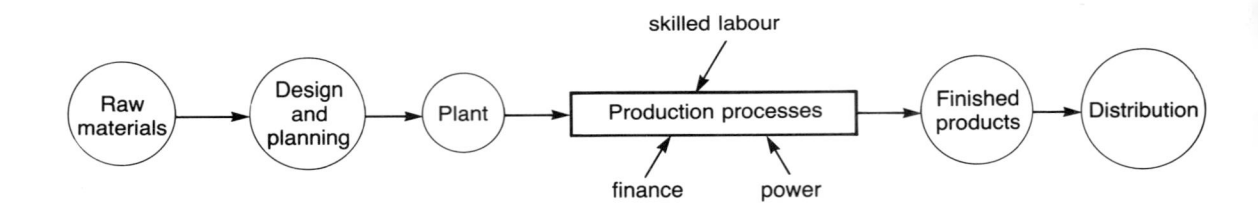

Location

We have looked at how goods are designed and produced. But we have ignored *where* they are produced. Any decision to build a new factory, or to expand an existing business involves a location, that is, where to build and develop.

Here are some of the factors to be considered when deciding on a location.

1 *The supply of raw materials*
Raw materials may come from overseas. Timber, iron ore, zinc and uranium have to be imported from abroad. Foodstuffs such as coffee, rice and fruit have to be brought in from South America, the Far East, Africa, the USA and Europe. Access to ports therefore is an important consideration.

If the raw materials are available in the UK, access to them is just as important. It may be essential to build a factory near to the main supplier of steel, wood, plastics, chemicals and other materials.

2 *The supply of components*
Components are parts of a finished product. For instance, car manufacturers need to buy tyres, windscreens, gearboxes and many other parts from specialist supply companies. It is necessary for these suppliers to be based near to the main manufacturers, which explains why many of the component companies are in the Midlands.

3 *Easy access*
The transport of materials and finished goods may be by train, road, air or sea. A major factor for any company, large or small, new or old, is easy access to raw materials, suppliers and customers. This could mean building a factory near Southampton, London, Liverpool or another port. Or near a main railway line, with safe goods yards. With the development of the motorway system, lorry fleets and a well-organised supply system, the managers of a company could decide that access to a motorway such as the M2 or M3 (easy access to the Channel ports), or to the M1 or M6 (linking north and south England) is more important than any other factor.

4 *Energy*

Where and how a firm gets its raw materials and components therefore influences the decision of the managers on where to build new factories or offices. A good example of this is in the oil industry, where Aberdeen, in north-east Scotland, is now a major centre because if its closeness to the North Sea oilfield.

In the past, a major factor was access to energy sources such as coal and gas. This explains why the shipbuilding, iron and steel and chemical industries grew up near to the major British coalfields. Today, with easy access to electricity and to nuclear power, the supply of *local* forms of energy is not so vital.

5 *Customers*

Another major factor is the location of customers, that is the buyers and users of the company's products. It may be vitally important to be near the main customers. For instance, the major reason for the concentration of financial and investment companies in the City of London is nearness to the head offices of the banks, the Bank of England and the Stock Exchange.

6 *Labour supply*

Manufacturing and service industries need skilled people. One of the most important factors for a firm is access to *sufficient people* with the *right skills*. Nowadays, the skills are likely to be in electronics rather than skills such as shipbuilding and machining. This has been a major problem in areas such as south Wales and north-east England where people were trained for traditional industries. When these declined, people were left with skills which were no longer needed.

However, there is a positive side to this development. American and Japanese companies which have set up manufacturing plants in the UK have begun to build their factories in Northern Ireland, Scotland, Wales and the north of England. They announced that a major reason for this decision was because of the supply of available local labour; people who were eager for jobs, and who already had good practical skills. Training these people in new technology was therefore quicker than training those who had no knowledge of any technology or engineering.

7 *Land*

If a company needs to expand, it may be impossible because no land is available to rent or buy nearby. This could mean looking for a 'green field' site elsewhere. This means building a new factory in a rural area, or at a 'new town' such as Milton Keynes, Cumbernauld or Peterborough.

8 *Tradition*

All the reasons mentioned so far are *economic* ones. But in the past (and today) there may be other factors involved. For instance, if someone thinks up a brilliant new idea and can develop it near to where he or she lives, it is possible that a new industry might start up there.

Another reason is that a group of foreign immigrants might settle in a particular area and start trading or manufacturing there. This happened in years gone by when French weavers, Dutch bulb-growers and Italian leather-workers settled in different areas of Britain.

9 *Government policy*

Another factor in considering location is the help given to companies by the government. In order to tempt firms to go to depressed areas of Britain, governments of both major political parties arranged schemes by which

The Japanese company Matsushita, the largest manufacturers of consumer and industrial electronic products in the world, set up in Cardiff some 12 years ago to manufacture Panasonic CTV products.

generous grants were paid to companies which moved production to these 'development areas'. This policy has been only partially successful, however, for managers are usually more influenced by the economic factors we have mentioned above than by local and central government grants.

Making the choice
Taking all these factors in turn, the managers of any expanding company face a set of difficult decisions.
- Suppose the source of raw materials and components is in a different region from the main bulk of their customers. Should the factory be put near the consumers or the suppliers?
- Should the company build a factory in a development area in order to take advantage of government grants, or ignore these in order to be near London and take advantage of trade with Europe, which could increase when the Channel tunnel is built?

The answers to these questions will lie in calculating *costs*. If raw materials are very bulky, the major cost may be in moving them to the manufacturing factory. If so, the managers are likely to build their new factory near to the source of raw materials. If, on the other hand, it is going to cost a lot more to take finished goods to the customers, the management might decide to bear the cost of transporting raw materials 200 or more miles to a factory next door to the main consumer market.

The Peterborough effect

Look at this advertisement. In your notebook, make a list of the factors which Peterborough offers to potential 'new developers'.

Assignment
1 Microtech is a company which makes microwave ovens, freezers and refrigerators. Most

---

PETERBOROVGH – ONLY THREE DAYS FORCED MARCH FROM LONDON.

Three days for the average Roman legionary, that is. It was the Romans who first put Peterborough on the map. Just 78 miles from central Londinium, straight up Ermine Street.

Nowadays the main road is the A1, and the journey time has been cut to under two hours. By train, Peterborough is only 50 minutes from the capital.

For those who would never have thought to look at the map, you'll find it placed neatly between the big cities of the Midlands and the expanding East Coast ports. The university city of Cambridge is also close by.

It's an ideal position, versatile enough to suit almost every kind of business.

Heathrow, Gatwick, Stansted and three other international airports are within two hours. Peterborough's own business airport handles private planes and executive jets.

Telecommunications are hard to better anywhere in Britain, and there's a whole infrastructure of advanced technology and computer services. Bringing Peterborough to within a micro-second of the world's major business centres.

The Romans, with their gift for a memorable turn of phrase, had a much simpler way of putting it.

All roads lead to Peterborough.

To find out why, return the coupon, or call John Bouldin on Peterborough (0733) 68931.

To: The Peterborough Development Corporation, Touthill Close, City Road, Peterborough PE1 1UJ. Please send me the Peterborough Information Pack.
Name _____ Company _____
Position in Company _____
Address _____
_____ Tel _____

DISCOVER THE PETERBOROVGH EFFECT. IT'S BEEN WORKING FOR CENTVRIES.

of its products were originally developed for the food processing industry based in Yorkshire where the head office and main factory are situated. However, the business has now developed so that most sales are to retailing chains such as John Lewis, Tesco and Bejam, to electricity showrooms, and to kitchen shops. The raw materials are mainly steel and plastics which are supplied locally.

A new factory is needed. Should it be near London where expensive land would have to be bought or rented but where the main buyers have their offices and warehouses, or in Leeds where there is plenty of land near the old factory and a good supply of labour?

Write, in order of priority, the reasons why you think the directors of Microtech should decide on London or Leeds.

2 Make a list of all the possible sources of power and energy for manufacturing industry in Britain.

3 The map shows the major UK motorways. Drivebox Floor Cleaners has its major factory at Warrington. What are the best possible methods of transport for this company's products to UK and overseas markets?

12
Manufacturing industry

What is *manufacturing*? One definition is that it is making things by using machines.

The three pictures on the next pages show three aspects of modern manufacturing techniques. Match the following descriptions to the pictures.
- a completely automated assembly line, making machine parts.
- mass produced biscuits in a food processing factory.
- growing millions of tomatoes under glass.

On the other hand, manufacturing could also be said to include two self-employed people who have converted a garden shed into a workshop where they design and sell ceramic jewellery.

Manufacturing, therefore, whether it is large-scale production or small-scale do-it-yourself, is the process of converting raw materials (which can be steel, wood, fabrics, plastics and many other materials) into finished products or parts of other people's products.

All around you there are articles which have been manufactured. Make a list of six items that have been made from each of these raw materials:

iron	leather	glass
wood	fibre	vegetable products

Manufacturing is the essential aspect, the key, to many companies. If we didn't make things to sell, there would be nothing for the sales, marketing, finance, personnel and other departments in a company to do! And if Britain didn't manufacture and sell goods abroad, there wouldn't be any money to pay for pensions, allowances, the health service and other social services. This is why any country's prosperity depends on making products and selling them.

Grubb's food processing company

Most of the workforce of a company is involved in manufacturing.

At Grubb's food processing factory there are 208 people. They are organised like this (the number of staff in each section is shown in brackets):

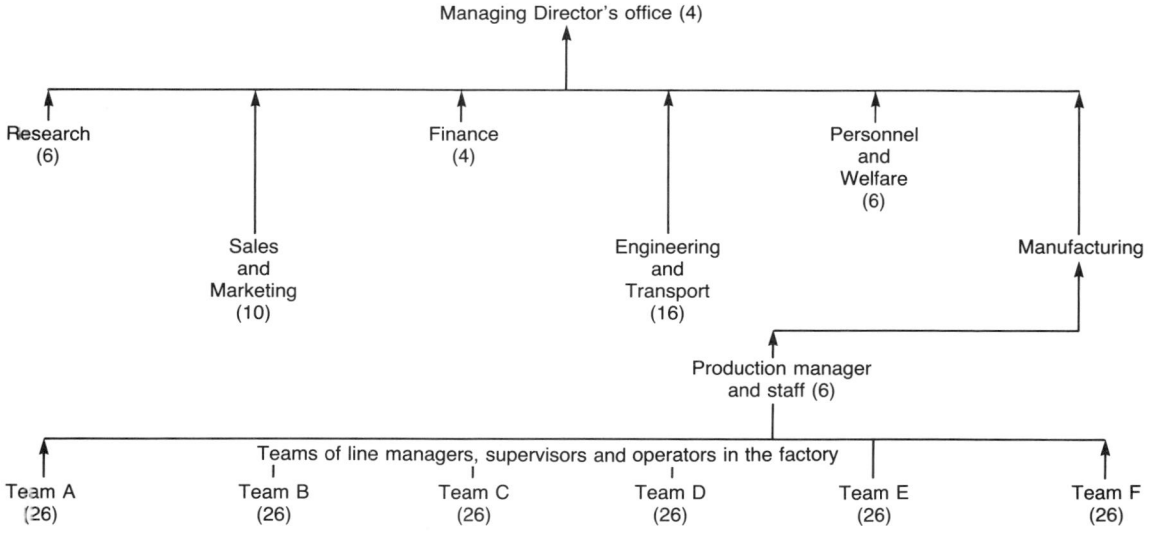

```
                        Managing Director's office (4)
                                    ↑
      ┌─────────┬─────────┬─────────┼─────────┬──────────┐
      ↑         ↑         ↑         ↑         ↑          ↑
   Research   Sales    Finance  Engineering Personnel Manufacturing
    (6)       and       (4)       and        and
            Marketing            Transport  Welfare
             (10)                  (16)       (6)
                                                ↑
                                    Production manager
                                       and staff (6)
                                              ↑
      ┌─────────┬─────────┬─────────┬─────────┬──────────┐
    Teams of line managers, supervisors and operators in the factory
      ↑         ↑         ↑         ↑         ↑          ↑
   Team A    Team B    Team C    Team D    Team E     Team F
    (26)     (26)      (26)      (26)      (26)       (26)
```

1 What is the total number of staff who work in administration (excluding the whole manufacturing department)?

2 How many people, including the production manager's team, work in manufacturing?

3 To whom does the production manager report?

4 The six teams are arranged in three shifts.

37

How many of the manufacturing staff will therefore be working on the 6 am to 2 pm shift, assuming that the production manager has two staff on duty for this shift?

In the factory

As you can see from the diagram on the previous page, the manufacturing department or section is headed by a senior manager. The job-title may be 'works manager', 'production manager', 'factory manager' or something similar.

Next in line are supervisors, foremen or women, and section heads. Each shift will have its own team leadership of these senior people.

When you visit a factory, you might discover that there are three main parts to the manufacturing team. These are engineering, production, and packing/distribution. Each one is closely linked to the other. The engineers are responsible for keeping the machines in good order. They have to be ready to deal with emergencies on equipment, power supplies, vehicles and other mechanical parts. The personnel and welfare section has to be ready to cope with any staffing problems, although this is often also the line manager's responsibility.

The main tasks of the manufacturing team in a factory are:
- to plan the work to a schedule based on speed and effficiency of production.
- to keep careful control over costs.
- to see that each product reaches the quality standard set for it.
- to avoid or reduce waste.
- to keep the machinery of production in good working order.
- to see that the staff are working effectively and that they enjoy job satisfaction.
- to bring in and use new technology when needed to improve production.

This isn't the end of the list. Can you think of any other tasks for the production team?

New technology

To be able to deal with production, staff have to be trained in technical skills. This training is done 'on the job', in training schools, and through further education colleges. The line managers and supervisors also need technical knowledge, but they also require skills to deal with people and to solve production problems that might arise.

As production lines become automated and computerised, managers and other staff have to cope with advanced technology, such as the use of robotic controls. One of the reasons for high unemployment is that as production has been automated, less people are needed.

An automated warehouse. What do you think is the purpose of the robot arm?

Large firms

In this book we have discussed several examples of small companies, that is those with under 100 employees. On the other hand, there are companies with thousands, even tens of thousands, of employees. In terms of what these companies are 'worth', the figures run into billions of pounds or dollars.

Multinational companies

These are firms which operate internationally, that is they have manufacturing plants in more than one country, and they attract investors (people who lend money) from all over the world. Among companies of this type are the big oil companies such as Shell, BP, Texaco, Gulf Oil. Also included are electronics firms such as Texas Instruments, IBM, Apple and Commodore. The headquarters of a multinational company could be anywhere – the USA, Britain, Switzerland, France, Japan. The main 'holding company' (that is, where the power really rests), is likely to be in a country such as the USA (for IBM), Japan (for Sony and National Panasonic) or Britain (for BP and ICI).

Another feature of these companies is that they will have manufacturing or assembly bases throughout the world. For instance, IBM make and assemble their computers and other business machines in the main western European countries and in Australia, South America and Japan. Therefore the workforce is huge, and the management of the company in one of these countries is almost independent of the holding company. Almost – but if things go wrong, the Japanese or American owners would be likely to 'jump on the backs' of the British managers.

Heavy industry

In this group are companies making large goods such as ships, cars, machinery and steel or large quantities of goods, biscuits and clothes. In Britain, they would include the British Steel Corporation, British Leyland, British Shipbuilders, Pilkington (glass-makers), Bowater (paper), British Aerospace (planes), Unilever (washing powders) and so on.

Here is a list of some British companies. Match the company to their major product, choosing from those in the list on the right.

1	MFI	A	advertising
2	Ferranti	B	oil
3	Bejam	C	baby clothes and household goods
4	United Biscuits		
5	Habitat Mothercare	D	frozen foods
6	BPCC	E	computers and electronics
7	Courtaulds	F	fertilisers
8	Britoil	G	furniture
9	Saatchi & Saatchi	H	locks and safes
10	Fisons	J	printing and publishing
11	Distillers	K	clothing
12	Chubb	L	food products
		M	whisky

Answers: 1G; 2E; 3D; 4L; 5C; 6J; 7K; 8B; 9A; 10F; 11M; 12H.

Changes in heavy industry

In the last fifty years there have been many changes in heavy industry.

Britain used to be the world leader in shipbuilding, coal, steel and machinery production. Now the leaders are the USA, Germany and Japan. British companies send their ships to be repaired in Finland, import coal from Poland, and buy fleets of Japanese cars for their sales staff. There are many reasons for this dramatic change in industry. In the first place, steel is made in huge quantities throughout the world: in fact, *too much* steel is made, so that companies cannot sell it! Cars and ships can be manufactured much more cheaply elsewhere. Coal has been challenged by other forms of power, such as oil, electricity and nuclear power.

The results of these changes have affected the traditional manufacturing areas of Britain.

Look at the map on the next page. It shows the main areas for steel and coal production and shipbuilding.

Questions

1. Where are the shipbuilding areas?
2. Two of the coalmining areas are missing from the following list. What are they: Kent, North-East England, Lancashire, Yorks and Derbyshire . . . and?
3. Name the three cities which were connected with steel-making.

The reason why the coal and steel industries were originally linked is that steel-making needs iron ore and coal-fired furnaces. Most of the iron was imported from other countries and arrived at ports such as Bristol, London, Liverpool, Glasgow and Newcastle. As British steel-making declined, men and women in their thousands lost their jobs, which is why these same areas have high unemployment figures and a history of industrial unrest.

people who are highly skilled in newer technologies – computers, electronics, telecommunications, chemicals, food processing, publishing, plastics. The raw materials for these industries are much easier to move around, and so are called 'light' industries.

The newer industries have developed near to their main markets which are in the south-east corner of Britain. The industries also need to be near ports and airports. Because Europe is the main market, the concentration has been on the eastern side of Britain, which hasn't done any good for Glasgow, Liverpool or Manchester.

The motorway network, too, is important. New companies look for easy access to main cities, and so they have grouped themselves along the motorways such as the M1 and M4.

The transport industry

All of these industries depend on transport. In the past, the main method of transport was by sea. Ships are still very important, for most of the raw materials (on which all industries depend) are brought by sea. This is why Bristol, Southampton, London and Liverpool are such busy cities.

Today, however, most of industry's raw materials come from Europe. For this reason, two other ports have become very important. These are Dover and Felixstowe, and if you look again at the map, you will understand why. These are 'on and off' ports where heavy container lorries can be transported by sea direct to and from Europe. These huge 'container' systems of transport, either by road or by rail, have brought about another kind of industrial revolution. One effect (and one that no one likes) is that heavy lorries thunder down the motorways and through towns on their way to the Channel ports. When the Channel tunnel is built, the traffic will increase.

Transport costs are high because the price of petrol is steadily rising. Therefore, new companies are tempted to build their workshops and factories near railway stations and motorways, and not too far from the south-east. All this accelerates the drift southwards of British industry, and adds to the gulf between 'north' and 'south'.

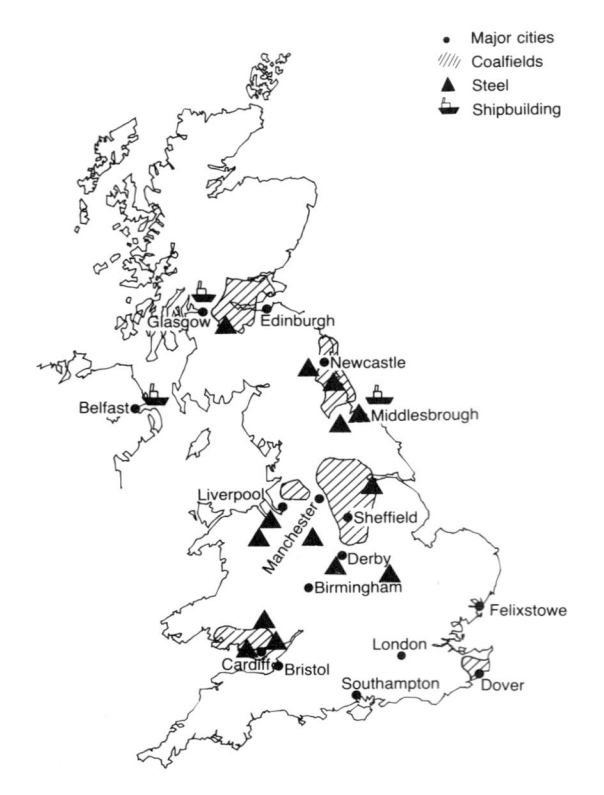

Later developments came when steel was made into cars, cookers, fridges, televisions and many more 'consumer' items. Factories had to have steel, but this could be brought from the ports quite easily. The car factories (and later electronics firms) were built near the main centres of population, to be near to their customers. This is the major reason why the car industry grew up in Birmingham, Dagenham (near London) and Coventry. Surrounding the huge car works were other industries which depended on them, such as tyres, machine tools, upholstery, electronics.

In the 1970s came another change. The big car companies found themselves in trouble, because cars were made more cheaply abroad and imported from France, Italy, Germany and Japan. As the sales of British cars declined, people in car companies and those dependent on them lost their jobs, too, and today there is much unemployment in the Midlands, around Birmingham and Wolverhampton, Liverpool and other parts of the north.

Light industry

As the older industries have declined, Britain has developed new ones. These employ fewer

Special development areas

Some parts of Britain badly hit by the economic factors described above have been designated by the Government as 'special development areas'. This means that the Government will pay generous grants to companies that build factories in these areas. However, a new firm will have to consider carefully its best option: would it be better to set up a factory in Wales, Northern Ireland, Scotland or north-east England and get the grants; or choose a site on the M4, between London and Bristol, much nearer to customers and with easy access to Europe?

Look at the advertisement. It is very skilfully written. It's written by an official of a development centre, and uses the example of a well-known and successful product.

Read the advert. What are the reasons why Mum Rollette went to Northumberland?

Advantages and problems of small, medium and large businesses

As you can see, the chart below is divided into three columns. Large companies are those with over 1000 employees and a turnover of over £10 million a year. A small company is defined as one with under 100 employees and a turnover of under £1 million a year. Anything in between is a medium-sized company.

On the left-hand side of the chart is a list of advantages and problems.

Copy the chart into your notebook. Then put a tick in the column if you think the particular problem or advantage is appropriate for a small, medium or large company. You could, of course, have ticks in each column, if you think it applies to all three companies.

Why keep Mum about Northumberland

It's no secret that investors have found the opportunities irresistable.

Bristol Myers, the American toiletries and pharmaceutical company and makers of 'Mum rollette', certainly think so. Explaining the setting up of its new UK manufacturing centre in Cramlington New Town Joe Brady, Managing Director, states "The decision to move our facilities was made after very careful consideration of the alternatives available. The Cramlington site will provide much improved working conditions as well as excellent amenities... The quality of industrial development in the area and excellent employee relations were also important factors in attracting us to Northumberland."

If you scent success have a quiet word with:
John Hamilton, Industrial Development Officer, Northumberland Business Centre, Southgate, Morpeth, Northumberland NE61 2EH. Tel: (0670) 514343. Telex: 537048.

Northumberland

Courtesy Northumberland County Council

Advantages and Problems	Large companies	Medium companies	Small companies
A *Production* can use mass production methods			
can respond quickly to market needs			
can specialise in one or two main products			
can accept last minute orders			
can make a standard product, and manufacture thousands of them			
can use a big sales force with a large advertising budget			
can take on large-scale market research			
B *Finance* can buy raw materials or products in bulk			
can negotiate big discounts on purchases			
uses computerised accounting and business systems			
can afford to reduce prices for most products			

41

can secure bank loans more easily
finds it difficult to borrow money

C *Personnel*

managers can deal personally with employees
staff all know each other
offers scope for different careers in the company
employs specialists
staff have to be able to do more than one job
can set up a profit-sharing scheme for employees

In your notebook, make a list of *other* problems, advantages and disadvantages of being a large, medium or small manufacturing company.

A study visit

You should try to arrange a visit to a local manufacturing company. Perhaps your college or school staff can make the arrangements for you.

When you go, find out the answers to these questions. If you can't set up a visit, write to a firm, asking for sales brochures and the annual report, and study the company's documents to answer the questions.

1. What are the main products?
2. What was the volume production of ten major products last year (that is, how many of each was made)?
3. What is the management structure? Draw a diagram to show it.
4. What raw materials are needed? Where do they come from?
5. Who plans production and how is it done? Draw a diagram to show the production methods.
6. Who is responsible for 'quality control' (this means making sure that every item meets quality standards)?
7. How is business obtained: where do the orders come from; what companies or customers buy the products?
8. By means of a diagram, trace the route of an order from the time it is received to packing and distribution.
9. What transport systems does the company use? How does it move its products to customers?
10. What trade unions are there? How many members are there for each union?
11. Is there an employee participation scheme? How does it work?
12. How are prices for the products decided?

13
Marketing

Marketing isn't just a fancy name for selling. There's a lot more to the process of marketing than sales. Marketing is concerned with the design, packaging, and naming of a product. It involves pricing and launching, promotion and public relations, advertising and competitions, as well as distribution and after-sales services.

For instance, a special price reduction in the supermarket is likely to be a marketing idea. Lymeswold cheese, new to Britain, was entirely an idea of a marketing team.

Marketing is often the first and the last link in the business scheme. As you have seen, the first stage is *market research* where opinion polls, top ten charts and newspaper circulation figures are considered. Staff have to find out where and when, and to whom, a product will sell. This task can come long before a product is manufactured or put on sale.

There are also other aspects to marketing. In a large company, the marketing section or department, reporting to the managing director, might have a chain of command and section organisation something like this:

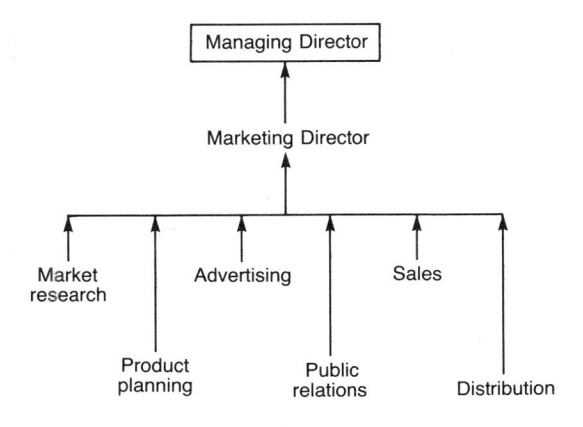

```
                Managing Director
                       ↑
                Marketing Director
                       ↑
    ┌──────────┬───────┴───────┬──────────┐
    ↑          ↑               ↑          ↑
  Market   Advertising       Sales
 research
            Product         Public
           planning        relations    Distribution
```

The job of the marketing director is to plan, organise and coordinate all these activities and sections.

Product planning

The work of the market research and product planning sections has been described earlier in this book. However, these sections have other duties which haven't been mentioned. Once a product has been decided on, these two sections are likely to be drawn into discussions on the *costs* of making it, and on the *packaging design* needed to make it attractive to customers. Once this is done, someone will ask 'what sales do you expect?' Accurate answers to this question are essential, for on it will depend how many items are made, and what the sale price should be.

Launching

The 'good news' of a new (or 'improved') product has to be carried to the eager, expectant public. There are many ways of doing this. Here are some of the main methods. Can you think of others? Write your ideas and suggestions in your notebook.

newspapers   television
magazines   posters

With a new idea or product, a company will often set a date for a 'launch'. This means that on, say, Wednesday 21 October, the news of a new car, soap, toothpaste, beer, newspaper, book, or whatever product is being launched, will be broadcast to the world. On this special day there may be all kinds of methods used to gain maximum publicity. These could be:

special offers : 'For one week only, two for the price of one!'
displays in shops : 'Come and see – and try for yourself – the full range of computers.'
a 'star' attraction : 'Smith's new store will be opened by Jimmy Savile.'
competitions : 'Let the *Mirror* make you a bingo millionaire.'

GRAND OPENING

CUT OUT AND KEEP THIS VOUCHER FOR **25p** *OFF ANY PURCHASE* IN NOVEMBER*
*Except Medicines and Prescriptions

SPECIAL OFFERS!

FREE Chablis & Smoked Salmon!

If you spend £250 or more with us on FURNITURE, CARPETS OR BEDDING we'll give you a presentation pack!

Sales

'Sales' is a word which describes many different kinds of jobs and activities. Here are some of them. See if you can add to the list.

shop assistant
supermarket cashier

petrol sales attendant
travelling sales representative

ice cream van driver
advertising manager

Some sales staff deal directly with the customer, as in shops. In other cases, sales are made by telephone, through advertising, by using special services such as retailers, and so on.

In a large international company such as Philips (makers of televisions, radios and other electronic goods) there are several departments each with managers and section heads. They work in teams, arranging sales in Britain, Europe and throughout the world. Their jobs involve:

- keeping in close touch with the retailers (the shops and stores where the goods are sold).
- planning a sales 'promotion' effort – that is putting in a lot of effort to sell, say, 200 000 televisions in one month.
- keeping customers informed about new developments, price changes, special offers, and other attractions.
- giving technical advice to customers and retailers.
- demonstrating the product at exhibitions and special events.
- providing an after-sales service.

In companies such as Rowntree Macintosh there are 'brand managers' whose job is to do all these jobs for only one product – a new chocolate bar, a special kind of children's sweet – or for a complete range of goods.

Now you try

Let's suppose you are planning a sales campaign for a clothing manufacturer, specialising in young people's clothes. It has been decided to launch a new line in matching jeans and shirts, suitable for both sexes, aged between 15 and 19.

Make a list of at least four ways by which the sales team could *attract the attention* of young people to this new product.

What *special events* can you think of which might be effective in stimulating sales?

What would be the best *sales outlets* (that is, shops, market stalls, mail order sales etc) for these goods?

Public relations

You will have noticed that public relations is an important part of the work of the marketing department. Public relations (PR) means giving the good news to the world, and the good news is that Company X is well managed, efficiently organised, caring, concerned with high standards of work, reliable, responsible . . . and so on.

The objective of this work is to maintain a good 'image' of the company in people's minds. You are more likely to buy from a company which you know (because you've been told) has a good reputation. Of course, it is no good having an effective PR department if the products, the goods, are not up to standard. Customers (that's you and me) aren't fooled for long by a lot of noise for a poor product!

One of the main tasks of the PR people is to keep the company's name constantly in people's minds. Again, this helps sales. The work of PR, therefore, is in producing and publishing press releases which give news about new products, special developments, prizes, stories about satisfied customers, and so on. A press release should contain a genuine story, otherwise no one will take any notice.

Other jobs done by the PR section are

mounting exhibitions, organising competitions, producing company magazines, arranging conferences and sponsored events. They are also required to boost the company name and slogan.

Slogans help us (the customer) remember the product or service. Can you recognise these? What do they remind you of?
- the listening bank
- it's gotta lotta bottle
- and all because the lady loves . . .
- refreshes the parts that other beers cannot reach
- the ultimate driving machine
- never knowingly undersold

Write your own press release

Suppose you are the PR person for a large store. This month you have to launch a new pram – more comfortable, safer and easier to wheel around.

A press release is needed – no more than 100 words. But first you have to find the story. It could be a 'bonny babies' competition. It could be a free pram to a deserving young Mum who normally couldn't afford one.

Anyway, make up the story or the 'event' and write your own press release.

Distribution

It is the task of the distribution section to see that the goods or services are delivered to the right customer at the right time.

This can be a complex task. Think of the problems involved in supplying hundreds of M & S or Sainsbury's branches with food and all the other products that are sold in these huge stores.

In order to deal with this job, the section may need a fleet of lorries and vans. It may need a system of ordering, using codes and computers. It may be involved in negotiations with shipping firms, airlines and lorry companies. It will certainly be involved in careful planning. If the distribution system fails, you know what happens when you go into the local store and ask for a packet of tea, the answer comes back, 'Sorry, we are right out of tea at the moment'.

When the packet of tea eventually reaches the shops, it could go into one of several kinds of *retailer*.

A retailer is a shop which deals directly with customers. Three types of shops are illustrated on this page. One is a large department store, such as Harrods, in London. Another is a *chain store*. (These are branches of a 'chain' of similar stores around the country, such as Littlewoods, British Home Stores and Tesco.) The third type is the 'corner shop', a shop owned by an independent shopkeeper. Sometimes the shopkeeper joins an association such as Mace or Spar to take advantage of special offers and lower prices, but he or she remains independent.

Which is which?

Which is the chain, the corner shop and the department store?

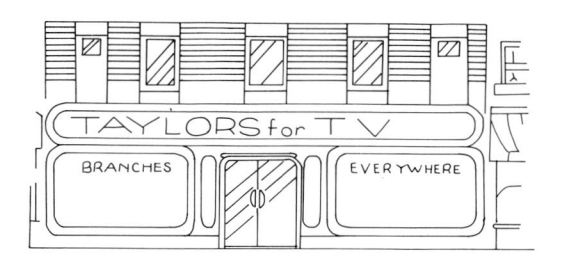

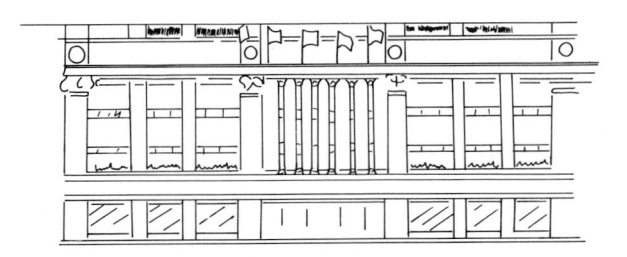

One important part of the work of the marketing department which we have not yet discussed – advertising – needs a chapter to itself.

14
Advertising

We all know what advertising is. After all, there's plenty of it. You see poster, cinema, television, newspaper and magazine advertising. You hear advertisements on commercial radio. Advertising is part of our daily lives.

Advertising is used to *sell* things. To be effective in this, it should:
- give *information* about the product or service.
- *persuade* people to buy or to take part.

First of all, there's the *message* or announcement. Then there is *payment*. Advertising isn't normally free, and the advertiser is prepared to pay to bring the news to the eyes and ears of the potential customer.

After that, there's persuasion. Is the advert *effective* in tempting people to buy or to give their support (to a good cause such as Oxfam), or to take part?

Advertising is such big business and needs so many skills (design, planning, the use of language) that many companies employ special advertising agencies to do the work for them. It is often these agencies which invent the slogans, the logo (the drawing and words used in a company name), and the full advertisement itself. Some company logos are shown on this page. Collect others, or draw examples of them.

The cartoon shows how one enterprising local couple used humour to attract customers.

Draw a cartoon or design a small advert for a business idea of your own, or to sell something.

I used to think...

...Dai John

played scrum-half for Wales...

until I discovered

Di & John's Health Food Shop

Who are the advertisers?

About 80 per cent of advertising is to sell products or goods. But this is only part of the story. Here is a list of advertisers and their reasons for advertising. Copy this table into your notebook and complete the third column with an example. The first one is done for you.

Advertiser	Reason for advertising	Company or organisation
charity	To appeal for money. To persuade people to offer practical help. To win sympathy for people in need.	Oxfam The Salvation Army Help the Aged
events organiser	To tell people about a sports event, a concert, an exhibition, a fund-raising village fair, a conference.	
government	A change in policy. New laws. To explain about local or government services. To discourage smoking and other health hazards.	
individuals	To rent or buy property. To sell or buy goods. To offer a service. To find a job. To announce a birth, a wedding or death.	
shops	To announce a special sale. To attract new customers for a special promotion.	
industry	To publicise a new product (car, food, fashion, holidays etc.) To sell the full range of goods or services. To recruit staff.	
A club or political party	To attract new members.	
Newspapers, TV, and magazines	To win more readers, viewers, advertisers.	

Leaflets and posters

Another method of advertising, used by small companies, is to design, print and distribute handbills or leaflets through letterboxes in the local area. Collect some of the handbills which are pushed through your letterbox. When you have studied them and thought about it, design and write a handbill or leaflet for a business idea you have in your head, or that you have heard about.

Effective advertising

For adverts to be *effective*, the words and pictures have to be put together very carefully. To attract attention and customers, they can be informative, inspiring, amusing, tempting.

The words used in an advert are called the *copy*. The pictures (drawings, cartoons, photographs, collages) are often called the *graphics*.

Examine the advertisement

Here are three exercises for you to try. When you have finished, you should have a better idea of how advertisers operate.

1 Collect together some newspapers and magazines. Read the copy.
   Which words are used most often? You will find that these words occur often: 'best', 'good', 'quality', 'new', 'value for money'.
   Make a list of other words and phrases often used by advertisers.
   Why are these words used?

Why is it that the words are effective?
Now look at the graphics.

What makes an advert attractive? Is it the use of the pictures? The use of colour? The people? The product itself, or the complete design of the ad?

2 Go to your local shop and buy a bar of chocolate or a packet of biscuits that you haven't tried before.

As you examine and eat it, analyse your reactions. Describe the packaging – colour, shape, feel, texture.

Take a bite. What about the taste? What words would you use to describe it?

Using the words you have thought about, write an advert for the product.

3 Here are two adverts. One is for a hairdresser in a small town. The other is an ad for Glasgow, using a modern hairstyle to attract attention. Are they effective ads? Explain how and why they are (or aren't) effective.

A FASHION CENTRE? GLASGOW?
SOME OF BRITAIN'S MOST AUDACIOUS DESIGNERS AND COIFFEURS COME FROM GLASGOW. WE LET KNIGHTSBRIDGE AND REGENT STREET SELL THE KILTS, WHILE OUR DESIGNERS ARE BUSY BUILDING THEIR OWN THRIVING BUSINESSES . . .

Need a haircut, shampoo, set or styling?

If you look like this when you pick up the phone, you ought to ring me immediately. Have your hair done in your own home.

Phone Vicky on 67834.

The message is in the picture

Effective advertising makes use of visuals or graphics. The objective is to capture attention, hold it, and reinforce the message of buy, buy or give, give. Look at the example of graphic advertising on the next page. We should explain that Horizon is a company which specialises in selling 'package holidays'.

What is the effect of the cartoon? Why are there so few words? What effect does the drawing have on you?

The expected reaction is amusement. The advertisers want you to think that it must be fun to go on holiday with Horizon. In any kind of communication between a *sender* and a *receiver* there should be a *message*. In this advertisement, the message is that there are plenty of laughs on a Horizon holiday with a company that is recognised all over the world, even by camels!

Now look at five different *colour* advertisements in magazines.

1 Write down what you think is the immediate effect of each one. Does the ad attract your attention. Does it hold your interest? Has colour been used to make the ad eye-catching? If so, how has colour aided the effect of the advert?

2 Next, watch five television adverts more closely than you might in normal circumstances. What makes these five effective? Is it the use made of drama, comedy, actors' voices, the dialogue or musical accompaniment, jokes, the speed of delivery of the lines . . . or what? Write down why you think

"Must be Horizon again"

each advert is effective . . . or why it is *not* effective.

The advertising business

The advertising business is made up of three groups of firms or organisations. They are:
- *the advertisers* – they spend the money on telling people about their goods and services.
- *the advertising agencies* – they advise the advertisers and produce material for them.
- *the advertising media* – they are the newspapers, television companies, and magazines which carry the message.

It could be said that there is a fourth group – you and me. We are the *target audience*. You will have noticed that most adverts are carefully designed to appeal to a certain kind of person – older people (for electric blankets!), younger people (fashion clothes, jeans etc), and special groups, such as motorists, gardeners, children etc.

Let's look at each of the groups in turn.

Advertisers

A recent newspaper analysis gave the names of the major advertising companies. They are all huge organisations. The names (such as Procter and Gamble) may not be known to you. But their products are, and some of them are listed below. The amounts of money spent on advertising are colossal. Notice, too, how influential television is – some companies concentrate entirely on TV advertising. But remember that a 30-second advert on TV costs about the same as a full-page display in a national newspaper. Television is effective if the advertiser wants to reach a huge audience for a product that will sell to most of them – holidays for instance. But if the advertiser is aiming for a section of the audience, let's say young people, the agency might advise putting full-page colour adverts in a wide range of teenage magazines. That would be cheaper and could be a lot more effective. The following table gives the main advertisers in the UK and a breakdown of the amount they spend on different types of advertising.

Company	Some products	Amount spent in £s a year	TV (% of total spent)	Press (% of total spent)
Procter and Gamble	Ariel, Bold, (shampoos)	50 million	98	2
Mars	Mars Bars, Bounty, Twix	30 million	98	2
Cadbury's	Dairy Milk, Crunchie, Flake	30 million	99	1
Imperial Tobacco	Cigarettes, cigars, tobacco	28 million	26	74
Kelloggs	Corn Flakes, Special K	26 million	96	4
Rowntree Macintosh	Yorkie, Aero, Kit-Kat	24 million	97	3
General Foods	Maxwell House coffee	21 million	98	2
Electricity Council	Central heating, cookers,	20 million	76	24
Pedigree Petfoods	Kit-e-Kat, Pedigree Chum	19 million	99	1
Nestlé	Nescafé, Crosse and Blackwell	18 million	90	10
Austin Rover	Metro, Maestro, Rover	16 million	40	60
Lever Brothers (Unilever)	Persil, Surf, Comfort	16 million	94	6
British Gas	Cookers, fridges, central heating	15 million	82	18
Van Den Berghs	Flora, Blue Band, Stork	15 million	84	16
Gallaher	Benson and Hedges cigarettes	15 million	36	64
Birds Eye	Fish fingers, beefburgers	15 million	95	5
Ford	Granada, Fiesta	15 million	50	50
Cooperative Society	Local shopping campaigns	14 million	35	65
Heinz	Baked beans, soups, baby food	14 million	84	16
Vauxhall	Astra, Cavalier	14 million	75	25

The agencies

Advertising is a very skilful job. The big agencies such as Saatchi & Saatchi employ market researchers, accounts managers, graphic designers and sales executives who buy 'space' on TV, radio and magazines for the lowest price they can negotiate. An agency (such as J. Walter Thompson, another large agency) might employ over 500 people, while a smaller one might have only a handful of staff. The volume of business is huge. A large agency might deal with £90 million of business in a year, and one contract might be worth £10 million a year, if advertisers such as British Telecom, Guinness or the Conservative Party come knocking at the door!

The advertising media

Remember that we said there were three main groups involved in advertising. The third is the 'media'. They are newspapers, magazines, television, radio etc.

If you look closely at your favourite magazine, you will find that it offers advertising space, but at a price. Television is by far the most expensive medium, and it can cost anything up to £30 000 for *one minute* of peak-time viewing (7 pm to 11 pm daily), and up to £10 000 for non-peak times. A half-page advert in a national newspaper, such as the *Daily Mirror* or *Daily Telegraph* can also cost £10 000. On the other hand, an advert in a local newspaper may cost something a lot more reasonable – £250 for a half-page. But how many more readers will the *Daily Express* reach than the *Frinton-on-Sea Focus*?

The public
Then there's us. We are the people in whom the advertisers and agencies are interested. To discover what people want, the agencies use market research techniques. They find out about the likes and dislikes of the general public, and build an advertising campaign around that knowledge.

As an exercise in seeing how advertising agencies pursue us, carry out an investigation of your own.

Over the course of a week or two, obtain copies of the main national and local newspapers. Copy and complete the chart giving the price, the circulation or average daily sales of each newspaper and the cost of a half-page advertisement. Also measure the total area of newsprint given to advertising and work out the proportion given to advertising for each newspaper. The first example in the chart is done for you.

6 Entertainment and tourism
7 Computers and electronic household goods
8 Clothing
9 Books, magazines, TV and newspapers
10 Shops, stores and other retail outlets for goods

Plan an advertising campaign
Let's see if you can plan and carry out an advertising campaign.

The product is a new magazine for young people. It will have features and articles about music, health, sport, fashion etc. But there's a lot of competition from other magazines. Take each step in turn.

- *Finding a market*
  Carry out some market research in your own school or among your friends. Find out why people buy magazines and what they like best about them. Is it stories about pop stars or groups, 'personal' problems, sporting stories . . . or what?
- *What's in a name*
  Invent your own name for this magazine. It has to be different from other teenage mags, so look at the competition. You will see many of these magazines on the shelves of a newsagent's shop or WH Smith.
- *Buy this . . .!*

Name	Price	Circulation	Cost of a full page	Proportion of advertisements
The Mail	20p	1.8 million	£18 000	40%

Below is a list of the 'top ten' products i.e. those on which the most money is spent on advertising. Look through your collection of newspapers again, or a set of magazines, and classify the adverts according to the top ten categories. See if your collection agrees with this chart.
1 Household and leisure goods
2 Food
3 Drink and tobacco
4 Cars and other vehicles
5 Toiletries and medical goods

Produce an attractive, informative and interesting single-page advertisement for the new magazine.
- *How much?*
  Now you have to decide on some business matters.
1 What price will you put on the magazine (again, check the competition)?
2 You have £100 000 to spend on advertising. How will you spend it?

15
Selling

Once goods are manufactured, marketed and advertised, they are put on sale. There are several ways of selling. Let's carry out a survey to find out how goods (and services) are bought and sold. **A** is a list of goods. **B** is a list of places where they could be bought. Match the two lists. You should discover that the same goods can be bought and sold in several of these places.

A	sweets	**B**	motorway service station
	cigarettes		discount store
	cars		corner shop
	computers		mail order
	newspapers		supermarket
	clothes		garage
	petrol		Woolworths
	bread		electrical goods shop
	shoes		department store
	furniture		hypermarket

Wholesalers

All of the sales outlets listed above are *retailers*. This means that they sell directly to the public. A manufacturer may sell goods directly to a retailer or may sell large quantities of stock to *wholesalers*.

Wholesalers are people who buy in bulk from several manufacturers and then sell in small quantities to retailers. This is a very important service. Suppose, for instance that you are the owner of a do-it-yourself shop. You could stock goods – tools, paint, wallpaper, timber – that are made by over fifty different manufacturers. If you had to deal with each manufacturer, you would spend a great deal of time on the telephone, filling in forms, doing a lot of paperwork. Wholesalers can help you to avoid all this work. Their business is to buy from all fifty manufacturers, store the tools and materials in their warehouse, and sell in small quantities to many different shops. The diagram (above right) shows how this process works.

Wholesale and retail prices

A price has to be paid for this service. Let's take an example.

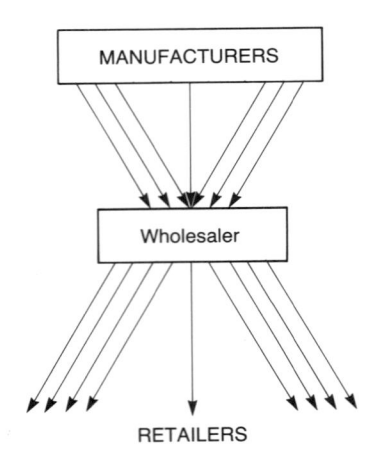

Suppose a manufacturer, let's call them 'Kitchens Supreme Ltd', builds kitchen units – cupboards, shelves, worktops etc. The company makes 2000 different units in a year. It sells to four major wholesalers, in blocks of 500 units. That's good business, because Kitchens Supreme have to deal with only four customers, so this cuts down on time and paperwork.

Then the wholesalers go to work. They sell directly to kitchen suppliers throughout the country – that is department stores, high street shops and so on. But at each stage, the manufacturer, wholesaler and retailer have to make a profit. Kitchens Supreme's price for a single unit is £100. That's what the wholesaler pays. But the wholesaler adds on £50 when selling to the high street store – price now £150. The retailer needs to make a profit, too, so adds another £40. The customer thus pays £190 for the kitchen unit.

In order to cut out both wholesalers and retailers, Kitchens Supreme Ltd might decide to deal directly with customers. This is called *direct selling* and is usually offered by an advertising campaign in national newspapers. Of course, advertising like this is very expensive, and the cost has to be added to the goods, so Kitchens Supreme find they can't sell at £100 a unit, but have to ask for £120. Even then, the customer could be in Newcastle, and the manufacturing factory in north London. So there's also the cost

SAVE UP TO 40% WITH BRITAIN'S BEST SELLING KITCHEN

KITCHENS SUPREME

PLUS A BUILT-IN LUXURY OVEN NORMALLY £500 — FREE

If you're looking for a new kitchen, there are a number of different ways you can go about it. Our way is the most direct. It offers free professional help with planning, delivery or installation within two to three weeks. And a saving of up to 40% on comparable kitchens. As you're about to discover.

The Complete Service

It sounds too good to be true. Doesn't it? Free planning from a professional consultant. Lightning delivery. And a massive saving on a superb craftsman-built kitchen.

So how do we do it? It's really very simple.

We supply our kitchens direct.

There are no middlemen to cause delays and push up prices. And we can look after our customers personally.

* Free planning by friendly professional consultants.
* This country's most advanced computerised kitchen service.
* A magnificent range of beautifully crafted kitchens.
* No waiting. No worries. Satisfaction guaranteed.

---

of transport. Before Kitchens Supreme can get their kitchen unit to the customer, therefore, it probably costs them £150. It might be better to go back to the stage when they sold to wholesalers and avoided all this extra work of advertising, transporting and dealing directly with customers. But Kitchens Supreme decide to give direct selling a try. An advertising campaign is planned. One of their adverts is shown above.

Study their advert and make a list of the *costs* of this venture.

First, there's the manufacturing cost, but they would have to absorb that cost anyway, whether they sold direct to the public or to a wholesaler.

What *additional* costs do they now have to meet? Clearly the actual advertising is one. What are the others? Make a list of the full *added costs*.

For and against wholesaling

You can now go on to complete these lists of the advantages and the disadvantages which wholesalers offer to manufacturers and the general public, in your notebook.

Advantages to manufacturers and customers
1. Wholesalers make the arrangements and pay for *transport* to retailers.
2. They are prepared to *store* goods, thus saving manufacturers the added costs of warehouse storage.
3. They buy in *bulk*, and *pay promptly*, so enabling the manufacturer to use this income to buy more materials and produce more goods.
4. Retail shops know they can obtain goods *quickly* from a central wholesaler's store, perhaps situated locally, without having to deal with many different manufacturers, perhaps spread throughout the country.

Disadvantages to manufacturers and customers
1. The consumer or customer at the end of the line pays a higher price because the wholesaler and retailer have both added a profit margin.
2. The manufacturer does not have direct contact with the customer. (On the other hand, this can be an advantage to a manufacturer!)

Once you've completed your lists you will notice that there are more advantages to having a wholesale service than disadvantages. It is often said that if the wholesaler was knocked out of the selling side of business, the price of goods would fall. But, as we have seen, this is not necessarily correct.

Retailers

Let us now look more closely at the different kinds of retailers which were listed at the beginning of this chapter.

Independents

These are the shops and stores owned independently, not part of large groups. For example, the corner shop, the sweet shop, the local butcher, the grocer.

The number of independents is slowly declining. Can you think of reasons for this? One of them is *competition*, mostly from big stores which have the buying power to negotiate discounts from suppliers.

There are advantages, however, in keeping corner shops in business. They are more likely to stay open late in the evenings, or to open up on Sundays. They often offer a free delivery service. The atmosphere is likely to be more relaxed than at a large store such as Sainsbury's. The owner of your local shop is likely to have time for a personal remark, a friendly greeting or a bit of advice about your needs and to remember you next time!

Multiple stores

These are stores which have many branches around the country, specialising in a particular line of goods. Among them are Barratt's (shoes), Burton (men's wear) and Holland and Barrett (health foods).

The main advantage to the customer of a store like this is the prices which it offers. The stores are often backed by a large group, with powerful purchasing power. They buy in large quantities and pay bills straightaway, which means that they can negotiate good discounts and pass some of the benefit to customers in lower prices.

Specialists in purchasing, store design, window-dressing and market research are employed by these stores. They keep themselves in the public eye by well-publicised regular sales and special offers.

There are plenty of examples of multiple stores in every large town. Next time you walk around the shopping centre, look out for them. Notice how they attract customers.

There are disadvantages, however, for the customer. Multiples tend to be in central shopping precincts: they may not be within easy distance of many customers. And because they are on central sites, it is likely that they will be paying high rents and rates. These charges affect prices, so, after all, there may not be too big a gap between the prices of the multiple and those of the corner shop.

Department stores

These include John Lewis, Debenham's, the famous Harrods store in London, and many more. Their big advantage is that many different goods can be purchased without having to move out of the shop. A 'department' can be as big (or a lot bigger) than many shops. Like the multiples, they can also negotiate discounts with suppliers because of their huge sales. This is one advantage to the customer. Another is that the stores are generally very large, so they carry a big stock of different goods, offering a choice of items. For example, a department store is a good place to buy furniture, because quite a lot of furniture is on display, and people can compare different styles and prices. Other attractive features of a big store are the 'extra' services such as rest-rooms, playrooms for children, a restaurant and cafeteria, lifts, a delivery service, and capable, experienced sales staff who have wide knowledge of goods in their department.

Payment is usually easy, too. Department stores accept credit cards, cheques, cash. They will arrange credit, so customers can buy now and pay later, through regular instalments. These are called budget or monthly customer accounts.

To bring the customers in off the street, these stores make a big effort to attract people. Window displays will be changed regularly, and are artistic and eye-catching. Notices announce 'reductions' and 'sales', with 'special offers'. At Christmas, Santa Claus will be available! All through the year, too, there may be exhibitions, a special opening with a television 'personality', demonstrations and free offers. Visiting a department store can be an entertainment in itself. But the objective of the sales staff is always the same – to persuade the customer to buy.

The main disadvantage is that the city site, with high rents and rates, has to be paid for, and the customer pays in the long run. Also, the store may not be easy to reach, and the car park may be some distance away.

Supermarkets and hypermarkets

Supermarkets are very popular with food-shoppers. Tesco, Asda and Sainsbury are prime examples. Shops such as these carry a wide range of goods, and the week's shopping can be completed in one visit. Self-service arrangements, with trolleys and baskets for everyone, are another feature.

Most of the goods in these shops are 'moved' rapidly. Frozen foods, bread, confectionery, toilet articles, washing powders, tinned foods and vegetables – these are the basic goods offered on supermarket shelves.

Again, as in the big stores, the managers of supermarkets buy in large quantities and can obtain substantial discounts. Part of the savings is passed on to the customer in cut-price 'offers'. Because of self-service methods of selection, the store can reduce the number of sales staff. Next time you are in a supermarket, notice that most of the staff are on the check-outs. There will be a manager, with an assistant or two, 'behind the scenes', and there will be staff to fill the shelves and to move goods from the warehouse to the store.

A hypermarket or 'superstore' is an even larger store. It is likely to be well out of the town centre, perhaps on the edge of the city, surrounded by vast car parks. These stores sell 'consumables' (goods which have to be sold quickly, such as food) and 'consumer durables' which are goods that don't perish such as furniture, electrical goods, tools and paint.

All the advantages that have been listed for the supermarket are also applicable to these stores. And there are other advantages – ease of access for cars, free parking, bigger range of goods, even lower prices (rents and rates might be lower on the edge of town).

Hypermarkets started in the USA and spread to France. In Britain, the idea caught on in the 1970s, and companies such as Woolworth and Tesco moved in. Another example is Savacentre, in which several companies join forces to build and run huge stores.

Discount stores
Comet and Argos are two well-known names for this kind of store. They sell mostly electrical goods direct to the public at discounted prices, that is anything between 5 and 50 per cent less than the retail price. They can do this because the service they offer is often basic. The store may be little more than a warehouse, with five or six salespeople selling across a counter. Nothing may be on display except a catalogue. The discount store assumes that people have examined the goods elsewhere (perhaps at a department store) and know what they want to buy. The customer buys the goods which are still packed in the carton, and drives away. Anything extra adds to the cost – delivery, after-sales service, a demonstration.

Mail order
This is direct selling again, with wholesalers omitted. Cataloguing mail order companies include Littlewoods, Janet Frazer and Kays, which trade through agents who apply for the catalogues.

An agent buys goods for herself and her customers who she chooses from her relatives, friends, neighbours, or colleagues at work. The agent receives commission, usually 10% cash or 12½% goods on each purchase.

Items in the major catalogues are illustrated, usually in full colour, and accurately described with details of price and weekly repayments. Typical repayment periods would be 20 or 38 weeks, depending on the cost of the item, without extra charge above the catalogue price.

Orders are placed by telephone or post and delivery is direct to the agent's door, by private delivery service or by post.

Many major catalogues, including Littlewoods, are members of the Mail Order Traders Association (MOTA) and abide by their terms, one of which is that goods may be returned in new condition within 14 days of delivery.

Another kind of direct selling by mail is through advertising in newspapers and magazines. Look out for adverts and see how they offer goods for sale by post, using credit cards.

What are the advantages of this kind of buying? For the consumer, there's the pleasure of being able to choose goods from home. Another big attraction is the availability of credit – goods can be obtained immediately and payment is delayed for months. However, there are disadvantages. One is that you can't actually see the goods before you buy them. What other disadvantages can you think of?

A survey of the retail trade

Having read and studied the characteristics of different kinds of retailers, we can now make a survey of the various methods of retail distribution.

Copy this chart into your notebook. Complete the chart, listing the advantages and disadvantages of each method of retailing for the customer and the manager of the retail organisation.

Type of retailer	Retailer		Consumer/Customer	
	Advantages	Disadvantages	Advantages	Disadvantages
independent shopkeeper				
multiple store				
department store				
supermarket				
hypermarket				
discount store				
mail order				

16
Company case-studies

A multiple retail company

Everyone knows Marks & Spencer (M & S). It is that familiar store where people buy their socks, sweaters, pyjamas, food and many other things. But what few people realise is the huge size and the success of M & S. Let's look at some of the facts about this company:

- M & S is Britain's biggest retail company.
- It has over 260 stores in the UK, and others in France, Belgium, the Irish Republic and Canada.
- The turnover of the group in 1984–5 was a colossal £3213 million.
- The company employs over 50 000 staff in the UK, and in the course of a year spends over £290 million on salaries, welfare and pensions.
- Over 700 other companies supply the St Michael trade brand of footware, clothing, food, wine, homeware and other goods: they employ another 120 000 people.
- As for customers, every week over 14 million customers step into M & S stores to buy one thing or another. Together they purchase one quarter of the whole UK sales of ladies trousers; one third of the total sales of underwear, pyjamas and nightdresses; one half of the sales of ladies' slips.

Products . . .

Here is a list of some of the goods sold in Marks & Spencer stores. Write the names of six different items sold under each heading.
1 Menswear
2 Children's wear
3 Ladies' fashions
4 Packaged food
5 Home furnishings and gifts
6 Lingerie and nightwear

. . . and Costs

For every £1 that goes into the till, only a few pence end up as profit. The £1 is divided like this:

73p – paid to suppliers to buy the ready-made merchandise sold in M & S stores.
11p – staff wages, benefits and profit-sharing payouts
6p – running costs (including transport, telephones, rates, heating, lighting etc – the M & S rates bill for 1984 was over £28 million).
10p – profit

From the 10p profit, however,
4p goes in taxes.
3p is paid out as dividends to shareholders.
3p is retained by the company for future development.

A typical branch of M & S, about 1926

Assignment

Read the information provided about Marks & Spencer, and answer these questions. (Lord Sieff is now President of the company: he took over this post in July 1984.)

1 *The Chairman's Statement*
Lord Sieff of Brimpton is the grandson of Michael Marks, the founder of M & S. The extract reproduced over the page is from his statement as Chairman of the company, made in the Annual Report of 31 March 1984.
(a) Who was the founder of Marks & Spencer?
(b) In which town was the first 'penny bazaar' set up?

Statement by the Chairman

One hundred years ago Michael Marks, my grandfather, an immigrant from Lithuania, set up his stall in Leeds Open Market with £5 loaned him by Isaac Dewhirst, a small textile wholesale merchant and manufacturer. I do not suppose that either foresaw what that market stall would become by 1984, one hundred years later.

Tom Spencer, Dewhirst's accountant, joined Michael Marks in 1894—hence the name Marks and Spencer. He died in 1905 and Michael in 1907. Simon Marks, Michael's son, and Israel Sieff, my father, Simon's lifelong friend, were the great builders of Marks and Spencer. Simon worked in Marks and Spencer 57 years and was Chairman for 48 years until his death in 1964. My father, first a non-executive director, joined Simon full time in 1926.

Theirs was a remarkable partnership; the talents of each complemented the other. They established a philosophy and principles which have been the foundations on which Marks and Spencer has been built and to which it owes its success and reputation. Teddy Sieff succeeded my father, and I followed Teddy as Chairman; we built on the principles our predecessors had established.

The main principles were and are:

1. To offer our customers a selected range of goods of high quality and good value.
2. To work in close co-operation with our suppliers to develop this catalogue.
3. Always to buy British providing the goods our British suppliers produce represent high quality and good value.
4. To develop and maintain good human relations with our staff, our suppliers, and our customers.

Our principles are sacrosanct, our policies flexible—which departments to expand, which to contract, what new departments to introduce, where to build stores and what their size should be.

We seek goods of high quality and good value; if we cannot find the quality we seek we would sooner be without the goods than knowingly sell inferior quality. Of course we make many mistakes, but one must not be afraid of making mistakes, providing the lessons are learnt.

We work closely with our suppliers, one of whom, Dewhirst, the Yorkshire clothing manufacturers, has supplied us continuously for one hundred years; 45 have supplied us for over 40 years and 134 for over 25 years. We and they together often work with the raw material supplier. Ours is a joint effort to satisfy our customers' demands. The majority of our suppliers are innovative and design-minded, and are imbued with the desire to make products of high quality and good value, whether clothing, other textile products, goods for the home, or foodstuffs.

We and our suppliers have jointly developed methods of quality control based on modern scientific and technological developments. The late Dr. Chaim Weizmann, scientist and statesman, showed Simon Marks and my father in the 1920's how scientific and technological developments could be applied to maintain and improve the quality of the most ordinary goods. Our technologists are active members of the buying teams, not backroom men and women. They work closely with our suppliers, most of whom have developed their own technological teams.

Statement by the Chairman *continued*

Simon Marks, over 60 years ago, made it a principle to have as much produced in Britain of the goods he sold as he could find; even in those days nearly 90% of what the modest Marks and Spencer chain sold was home produced. Today some 90% of all our textile goods, and the food that can be grown in temperate climates is produced at home. We have found in most cases that this country can produce high quality goods equal or better than anything produced abroad.

A business is only as good as the people who work in it. In this day and age democracy, as we understand it, will only survive and flourish if we have a dynamic free enterprise sector within the mixed economy, and a dynamic free enterprise sector largely depends upon the attitude and commitment of all employees.

We started some 60 years ago to implement dynamically a policy of good human relations at work; this means more than paying good wages. It entails concern for the wellbeing and progress of everyone and treating everyone as an individual and with respect, talking to them and hearing what they have to say. We have 900 people in our Personnel Department, the majority of whom are spread throughout stores as staff management to look after, train, and encourage all employees.

Over the years we have built up our staff benefits to include non-contributory pensions, profit sharing, extensive health and welfare services, good subsidised meals, hairdressing and chiropody services. They are much appreciated; the majority of our staff are dedicated, hardworking and very productive. Morale is high and customer service generally good. We have over these many years built up within the organisation a Marks and Spencer family spirit, and many employees consider themselves partners as well.

Like many successful firms, we give to worthwhile causes, but have found that the cheque book is not enough. Many staff at Head Office and in the stores are actively involved in the communities in which we operate and trade. We have at present 14 people seconded to community projects for periods lasting between six months and three years, mainly on assignments concerned with job creation and youth training. They do not solve problems but they help to alleviate them, and during these secondments they learn much which stands them in good stead when they return to the business.

In my 12 years as Chairman I have been supported by a first class team of colleagues who understand and implement successfully the principles of the business. We enjoy first class co-operation from our suppliers of goods and services.

The business is in good shape but there is much scope for improvement. I hand over at the annual general meeting to Lord Rayner. He and I have worked closely together for 30 years; he has made a major contribution to our progress and I have no doubt he will lead the business to further success.

I thank all my colleagues and friends at Head Office, at stores and at our suppliers, for their close co-operation and help and our customers for their friendly support over many years.

Sieff of Brimpton

(c) What was special about Isaac Dewhirst in 1884, and in 1984?

(d) From what you have read, what would you say are *six* main principles of M & S business objectives and methods? Make a list of the six.

(e) What proportion of M & S goods are made in Britain? What do you think are the advantages and disadvantages of this decision?

(f) What has M & S done to improve the working conditions and benefits for staff? Make a list.

2 *A team effort*

In your own words, describe the jobs of these people who work in or for M & S:

selector
merchandiser
technologist
supplier
personnel officer

A team effort

Stores are continuously visited by head office staff concerned with getting the right merchandise in the right place at the right time.

They are members of a team from the buying departments: selectors, merchandisers, distributors and technologists.

The selector's job is to create an attractive range of merchandise. In fashions, ideas will come from a variety of sources: fashion shows at home and abroad, and from ideas submitted by the company's and suppliers' own designers. Often a new style is developed by combining the best features from several different samples.

In foods, ideas might come from the company's own experimental kitchens, from customers, staff or suppliers.

The merchandiser is responsible for deciding quantities, and arranging production. And it is the job of the technologist to ensure that the standards set by the company to its suppliers are met and maintained in every detail. This includes the number of stitches to an inch, the exact amount of meat in a pie or even the precise diet of chickens.

The buying teams work very closely with suppliers who are completely involved in the development and quality control of goods. The suppliers themselves frequently visit stores to check on how their products are selling.

This special relationship with suppliers has often been summed up as 'M&S being a manufacturer without factories and its manufacturers being retailers without shops'.

17
Multinational companies

A multinational company operates in several countries of the world. It has its headquarters in one of them; e.g. USA, UK, West Germany, Switzerland, Japan etc, with separate but linked offshoot companies elsewhere.

For example, IBM, the American business machines and computer company has IBM (UK) as one of its offshoots, and similar companies in Europe, South America and the Far East.

The parent company

There are several reasons why international companies operate in this way.

1 *To manufacture products or assemble them within the market*
It is likely to be much *cheaper* to make or assemble parts locally of motor cars, computers, fridges and other goods than to transport them perhaps thousands of miles across oceans.

2 *Lower wage rates*
In the Far East, wages are much lower than in western Europe and the USA, so it is much *less costly* to make e.g. electrical goods, clothes, toys and kitchenware in countries such as Korea, Taiwan and Singapore, and then export them across the world.

3 *Financial help*
Foreign companies setting up a factory in Britain can take advantage of the British Government's policy of *financial help* to companies that take over factories in development areas such as Northern Ireland, Wales and north-east England. For this (and other) reasons, Japanese, American, French and West German companies have formed UK companies and established manufacturing plants in the UK.

Assignment

This chart lists ten multinational companies. The first entry has been completed for you. Copy and complete the chart.

Company	Country of origin	Main products
IBM	USA	Business machines and computers
Texaco		
Unilever		
Philips		
Peugeot		
Rank Xerox		
Kodak		
McDonald		
Sony		
Hilton		

The host country

Many countries (including the UK) encourage multinational organisations to set up business in the host country. Again there are advantages and disadvantages with this policy.

One of the advantages is that it creates more jobs. For instance, a Japanese car company's new factory in Sunderland, on the north-east coast of England, will create 800 new jobs in an area where unemployment is 24% of the adult population who are eligible to work.

Can you think of other advantages to the host country? Make a list of them.

There are also *disadvantages*. One is that a multinational company might not create many (or any) jobs. Instead, they could import complete units (such as cameras, microcomputers, washing machines and hundreds of other articles) from abroad. This would damage the industry of the host country, especially if the goods from abroad were considerably cheaper (because of lower labour costs).

A second weakness or danger for the host country is that some of the profits of the multinational company could be sent out of the country and back to the parent nation.

To satisfy the host country, the multinationals plough some of their profits back into the economy by expanding their original business and developing new ones.

Can you think of other disadvantages for the host country and how they might be overcome?

Esso

Esso is a multinational organisation. Esso supplies energy and chemicals to countries across the world. Its principal activities are the exploration, production, transportation and sale of oil and gas, and the refining, distribution and marketing of petroleum products.

Put another way, Esso is concerned with:
- exploring for oil and gas in the North Sea and elsewhere.
- transporting crude oil from the North Sea by means of a fleet of ships.
- refining oil into many products including petrol, chemicals, central heating oil, fuel for electricity stations and many industries.

Esso's customers are 3000 industrial and commercial companies (and another 122 000 customers who buy through Esso's distributors), government departments and overseas countries.

Esso UK plc is vastly wealthy. For instance in 1984 the UK company invested £4500 million in its UK operations. It employs 6600 people. Gross revenue for its business in 1984 was £7845 million. Tax charges, paid to the UK Government, totalled £1463 million, 39% higher than in the previous year. Esso UK plc is only *one* of the Esso group of companies.

Amanda Stevens, shift supervisor

Exxon Corporation is the parent company of the worldwide Esso Group. Its interests are in oil, gas, chemicals and coal. Affiliated companies and divisions of the Exxon Corporation operate in the USA and in over 80 other countries.

Esso dates from 1888 when, as the Anglo-American Oil Company, it started exploring for oil and refining it. Today, it consists of a holding company, Esso UK plc, with two operating companies called Esso Exploration and Production UK Ltd, responsible for crude oil and natural gas, and the Esso Petroleum Company Ltd which is responsible for the refining, distribution and marketing of petroleum products throughout the UK.

Remember that this huge and powerful UK group of companies is only part of a worldwide Group, led by Exxon. To find out more about this multinational company you should write to Esso for free booklets about their work and activities: Corporate Affairs Department, Esso UK plc, Esso House, Victoria St, London SW1E 5JW.

Suppliers and consumers

18
Supply and demand

Demand

This is the total amount of a particular product which customers wish to purchase (and have the money to do so) over a period of time.

For example, the demand for new motor cars might be 100 000 cars over, say, a six month period. This means that all the manufacturers, both UK and overseas, are bidding to secure a percentage of the total demand. If one manufacturer, say Ford, secures 18% of the sales of new cars, it will mean all the other manufacturers, from Jaguar to Datsun, will be fighting for the remaining 82%.

Supply

This is the total amount of a particular product which all suppliers can provide. Supply can of course be increased if manufacturers make more of the product so in economic terms, supply follows demand.

Increasing demand

Demand is influenced by many factors. Among them are these.

1 *Price*
- Suppose all motor car prices were suddenly reduced by 20%. What would be the likely effect on the demand for cars, now at 100 000?
- Suppose the price of petrol was suddenly doubled as a result of a new government tax. What effect would this have on the market demand?
- Now suppose that car prices were increased by 20% for overseas manufacturers and importers, and there was no increase for UK car makers. What would be the effect of this on demand?

2 *Fashion*
Another way that demand can alter is by changing fashions. An example was in the sale of jeans. In 1979 flared jeans were very popular. Then, suddenly, the fashion changed and 'drainpipes' were 'in'. Overnight, shops were left with thousands of pairs of flared jeans that no one wanted.

3 *Customers' habits*
The way of life and the habits of customers can also influence demand. For example, the sales of double glazing improved dramatically because advertisers of double glazing emphasised the safety aspect (it is more difficult for burglars to break double glazed windows), and the cost benefits (reductions in heating bills).

4 *New 'improved' products*
Manufacturers constantly try to expand the sales market (that is, to increase demand) by improving on their products. You see this in

So mild you can wash your hair as often as you like.

As mild as only nature can be – Timotei shampoo. Containing natural herb extracts Timotei cleans your hair gently, leaving it soft and shiny with the fresh smell of summer meadows.

Timotei is perfect for every kind of hair – so mild you can wash your hair as often as you like.

Product Information – Timotei shampoo has been shown in scientific tests to be mild to both skin and hair. The pH-value, about 6, is close to that of normal skin.

---

advertisements for computers, for skin-care creams, for washing-up powders and detergents, and for many other products.

Let's look at one product – shampoos. The demand for shampoos would seem to be fairly constant. But there's one way that manufacturers might stimulate demand – and that's by persuading people to wash their hair more regularly. Also, if the manufacturers suggest that there's a 'hidden' or 'secret' ingredient (with 'special biological action') it might persuade people to buy more of their shampoo. For example shampoos are produced which are said to fight baldness, dry hair, greasy hair, 'flyaway' hair and all the other things thought up by skilful product developers.

Can you think of other reasons for changes in demand?

Price-elasticity

As we have seen, one way of increasing demand is by changing prices. A price reduction leads to greater demand. However, things aren't always simple. The demand for washing-up liquids, powders and detergents isn't going to change dramatically, no matter how hard manufacturers try to persuade us to wash our clothes, dishes and ourselves more often. The demand is said to be 'inelastic' or 'fixed'.

As it happens, the manufacture of these products is in the hands of a few companies, led by Proctor and Gamble and Lever Bros. The only way that one of these companies can increase sales is by selling more of Daz, Ariel, Domestos, Ajax or whatever, at the expense of other manufacturers. The demand for one of these products might be more elastic, because it is suddenly popular. 'Bio-Germ destroys all known germs' might persuade customers to buy it. But, before long, the other makers of detergents will catch up again, as they invent a new advertising slogan or 'catchy' jingle.

Price-competition

If we continue with the example of the washing-up materials, one way that the sales of Ariel might improve is if the price was cut. What would then happen is that the rival companies would cut their price accordingly. There would be a 'cut-price war'. Customers would benefit, of course, from the reduced prices. But the manufacturers would be making very little profit.

So, where there are only a few manufacturers, they keep their prices roughly equal – they don't go in for price-cutting wars. But this policy doesn't always work. For example, let us look at video recorders.

Overseas companies are prepared to go in for price-cutting to seize a larger share of the market for video recorders, so the price is elastic. If prices are reduced, more people might buy one. So the demand is elastic too. In this case, we could expect some price-cutting. But if you look at the prices of video recorders in the shops, you will find that they are very close. Again, therefore, it looks as if the manufacturers have kept their prices stable.

Questions

Discuss these questions in class or in groups.
1 Why do companies try to keep prices high? How do they do it?
2 How do firms try to expand demand? Which methods are seen to be successful?
3 Suppose the government thought that companies were keeping prices too high. What action could a government take to reduce prices?
4 How do companies deal with the changing pattern of demand?
5 Suppose that supply outruns demand, which means that firms are producing too many of a particular product. What should they do in this situation?
6 How do these policies (of stimulating demand and supply) affect *consumers*?

19
More turnover and bigger profits

As a company expands, the minds of its directors turn towards bigger turnover and profits. This is not greed. Nor is it planning for a rainy day.

There are several ways that profits can be used for the benefit of everyone – managers, owners, shareholders, staff, customers. Profits can help to:
- buy new equipment or land.
- build another factory.
- increase production.
- invest in research for future products.
- pay bonuses to staff.
- pay dividends to shareholders and thus encourage more people to buy shares in the company.

Value analysis

Assuming that a company wants to increase its profits, what action does it take to do so? Here are some possibilities:
- increase production in order to manufacture and sell more products.
- increase prices.
- reduce costs.

Can you think of any other ways of increasing turnover and profits? What problems will arise if any of these decisions are put into operation?

In industry and commerce, the methods by which companies decide on which (if any) steps should be taken is called *value analysis*. The managers consider the reasons why their product has value for customers, and how they could manufacture it more cheaply and yet retain its original value.
- Can the product be made more cheaply?
- If the answer is 'yes', how can it be done?
- Can cheaper materials be bought?
- Is it possible to employ fewer workers to make the same product?
- Can component parts be bought more cheaply in bulk (that is, 10 000 a time instead of 1000, at a lower unit cost)?
- Will component or parts manufacturers lower their prices: if not, can we find alternative – and cheaper – suppliers?
- Can the design be changed in order to reduce wastage of materials used during manufacture?

There are many other aspects of value analysis, but first let us look at a real example.

Best foot forward

W.A. Lees Ltd has made shoes, slippers and industrial boots for over a hundred years. In 1975, the company launched a new line of walking shoes and climbing boots called Tuffsoles which were guaranteed to last for years.

After a good start, sales and profits declined. In 1984 the managers carried out a detailed value analysis and market research project. They found that Tuffsoles were highly thought of by customers. They were strong and reliable and they lasted well, even with heavy use. As many people reported to the researchers: 'With a pair of Tuffsoles, you know you won't need to buy any more boots for years'. This is the kind of remark that alarms sales reps!

When the team looked at the competition, their hearts sank to their boots (sorry!). Footware from Italy, Spain and the Far East was lighter in weight, more flexible, and combined comfort with style. Imported shoes and boots were also an average 15 per cent cheaper.

The manufacturers decided to attack the competition.

But first they had two problems to solve.

Design

They teamed up with shoe designers who had fresh ideas. They decided on a completely new approach. To capture the youth market, the footware must have style. New materials and techniques would be used. At the same time, W.A. Lees Ltd didn't have money to buy new equipment. The new boots had to be made on existing machines and with the same (but reduced numbers) of staff.

The new styles – ankle boots, trainers and lightweight shoes – were all based on a flexible, one-piece moulded sole that gave low weight and good grip. The uppers were in leather or suede. Finally, a new trade name was invented – Superboots.

Finance

The designers, the company's buyer and the accountant came up with some challenging figures. Substantial savings could be achieved by:

	Savings
• cutting and moulding for one-piece production of the shoes and boots.	7.0%
• changing to a new lining which keeps out rain but lets the feet breathe.	2.2%
• reducing the number of eyelets.	0.8%
• using cheaper nylon laces instead of the traditional leather ones.	1.2%
• reducing staff by 15 per cent, because production processes are fewer and simpler.	5.5%
Total savings of	16.7%

With these reduced costs and new methods of production for Superboots, retail prices were fixed at £33 to £43, about the same prices as imported footware of the same quality. W.A. Lees Ltd is now looking forward to increase production and bigger profits.

Increase sales

Superboots is an example of increasing business by the introduction of newly designed products and by reducing costs. The more usual method of expanding business and profits is by increasing sales. But how is this done?

The usual way is to sell more of the same product. The starting point is likely to be the home (UK) market. This means that more money has to be spent on advertising; it may mean increasing the size of the sales team, with more frequent calls on customers. If successful, it could mean additional production, and could lead to a demand for more machinery and staff. The manufacturer is therefore increasing the *costs* as well as the *income*. As long as there is a good profit on increased sales, taking into account increased costs, the business will continue to do well.

The next business problem to arise may be *saturation*. If the company is making bread, there's no problem. The production line never stops, as long as people buy and eat bread. The same is true of all *consumables*. These are goods (such as food) which are used up as fast as they are produced. The market for these goods is never saturated.

But if the company produces *durables*, that is products which last for a long time, there may be a major problem. Durables are products like carpets, furniture, machines – articles which are bought to last. *Semi-durables* are products like clothes, (a jumper lasts longer than washing powder but not as long as a car), that is they lie halfway between consumables and durables. If a company has invested in mass production (machinery, staff, premises) to produce, say, televisions, what happens if almost every household has one? We then say that the market is *saturated*.

What do we do now?

Suppose you are the managing director of a company making microcomputers. Apart from the other 43 or so companies (at the last count) who also manufacture micros (the *competition*), there's a great need for us to expand our sales. One reason is to generate enough money to pay for the research for the next stage of computer development. So, what's to be done?

1 *Move in on your customers*
The sales team have already sold to 5000 customers. They discover that most sales are of one or two micros. Get your sales team to return to these customers to try to persuade them to buy another one or two, or better still, whole systems.

2 *Move in on your competitors*
Call on your advertising agency. Tell them that the next campaign must be to expand at the expense of the competition. (You'll occasionally see some TV adverts taking this line: 'our motorised lawnmowers are faster, cleaner and cheaper than "hovers". In newspapers, too, you'll see car manufacturers competing for business with cars that have the lowest petrol consumption or the best re-sale value, and so on.)

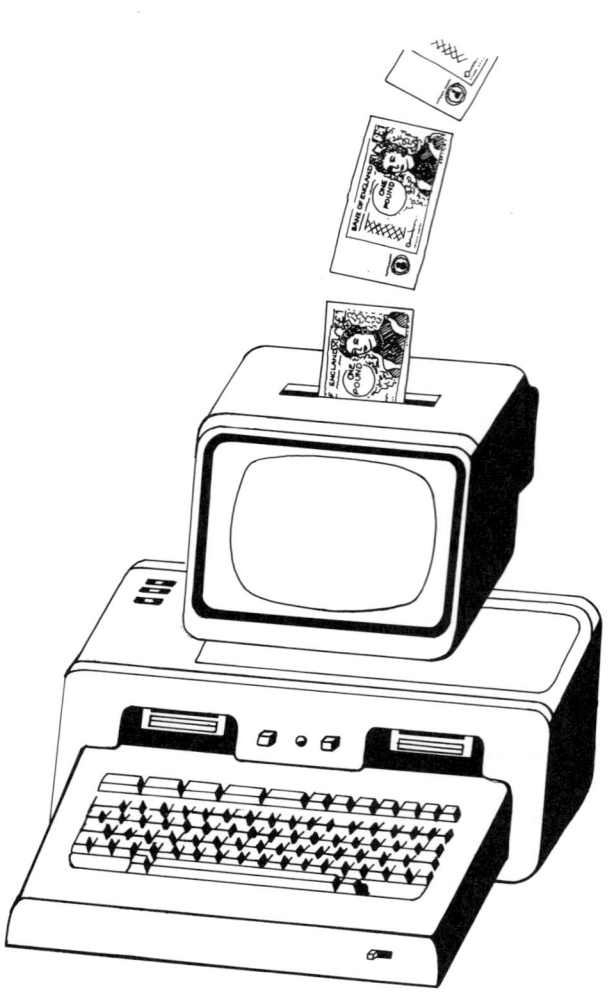

3 *Find new markets*
Apart from your 5000 known UK customers, there must be lots of other people 'out there' desperate to buy your micro. Get to them. There may be other UK companies that have never considered using micros, or they may be overseas, which means trying harder for export sales.

4 *Change the fashion*
Yesterday's fashions are today's dead sales. In the clothing industry ('rag trade') changes in fashions stimulate a fresh wave of buying. A different phenomenon applies to electrical goods where the manufacturer 'improves' the product each year, by adding something new. Yesterday's purchase is therefore *obsolete* (out-of-date). Your company could add colour or graphics or new software to your machine, and so grab more of the market.

5 *Make the product less durable*
One way of making sure that durable goods don't last *too long* is to deliberately use materials which deteriorate. For instance, some manufacturers have been known to use plastics which discolour. Motor car makers could use superior steel that doesn't rust! Electric light bulbs could last longer!

6 *Keep repair bills high*
A machine can be constructed so that if one part breaks or fails, then the whole unit has to be replaced. The reason is that to dismantle the machine to replace the part costs almost as much as the whole machine. For example, if a part of a clutch or a gearbox fails in a car, the garage mechanic will always say, 'it's got to be completely replaced', so the customer ends up by buying a new clutch or gearbox.

7 *Reduce prices*
We have already pointed out that one way of improving profits is to *increase prices*. Another way may be to *reduce* prices. This is the reasoning which lies behind the 'January Sales' campaigns of large stores in every town and city. The reasons are, firstly, that the 'sales' attract customers who are likely to buy more than one article: thus volume sales are greatly improved (in 1985 Harrods in London took £26 million in revenue in the January sales). Secondly, although prices may be cut by up to 50 per cent (very attractive to customers) the stores are still making a profit. Thirdly, 'sales' clear out old stock (which costs the company money to store) and gives space for the new season's stock.

Assignments

This chapter has looked at some of the ways by which firms try to increase their turnover and profits. Follow it up with these assignments which will give you an insight into how they do it.

1. Look in magazines and analyse some TV adverts to discover examples of these methods of stimulating sales. In your notebook explain (with illustrations) their effectiveness (or criticise them if they are not effective):
   (a) persuading people to buy more than one of a product.
   (b) comparing one maker's products with those of a rival.
   (c) changes in fashion.
   (d) 'new and improved' products.
   (e) costly replacements or repairs.

2. Suppose you are the managing director of companies making these goods. Suggest ways by which sales might be stimulated:
   (a) cycles.
   (b) children's toys.
   (c) wheelbarrows and garden tools.
   (d) fashion clothing for men and women.

20
Protecting the consumer

As we have seen, there are many ways by which manufacturers and traders can increase their sales. In this chapter we shall look at how these methods affect the buyer — the consumer — and how he or she can be protected.

The vast majority of companies are honest. They do not try to mislead or deceive customers. Their goods work properly and they give good service. On the other hand, there are people who are dishonest. They try to sell by any means possible, including telling lies. There are very few of them, and sooner or later the police catch up with them.

There are often exaggerated or wild statements made about goods or services. Some of them have become the basis for jokes:

On occasions you will read or hear about a newspaper, radio or TV team of investigators who have tracked down a dishonest company. Most of these stories start with customers' complaints that they have been deceived by false advertising.

Over the last 20 years, governments have taken steps to protect the public.
For example, laws have ensured that:
- consumers must not be deceived by advertising.
- goods that are sold must be in good condition and be fit for the purpose for which they are sold.
- goods should correspond to their description.

Fair trading and trades descriptions

In 1973, the Fair Trading Act set up a new department, the Office of Fair Trading. The job of its officials is to see that the interests of consumers are properly protected. If anyone has a complaint, they can contact the office (in London) or the Trading Standards Officer(s) at their local council.

The basic law which applies to nearly every buying and selling deal is an old one, the Sale of Goods Act, 1893. The Trades Descriptions Act, 1968 strengthened this law. Between them, they say:

- The goods you buy must be in good condition. This means that if they are broken or have parts missing, you are entitled to your money back. However, if the trader points out the defect e.g. 'There's a deep scratch on this television cabinet' you can't get your money back, but you certainly would if the set didn't work.

- The goods have to be fit for their purpose. This means that if you are sold oil for a lawnmower which is heavy engine oil and clogs up the works, you can get your money back — and you should be able to get the supplier to have your mower cleaned. If, on the other hand, you just bought any oil and didn't ask the trader's advice, you have no one to blame but yourself.

- The description of the goods must be accurate. If a label on a jumper says 'blue' and you discover when you get it home it's black, you are entitled to return the jumper and get your money back.

There are exceptions to these rules. For example, if you buy at an auction sale you are likely to find that you can't return the goods. It is recognised that auctions involve risks for a buyer. Nor do the three rights mentioned above apply if you buy from a private person.

The Trades Descriptions Act went further in defining buyers' rights:
- If a seller makes an untrue statement either in writing or verbally, then this is an offence and can end in a fine or prison. There have been many cases involving car mileage: by law the car dealer must tell you if the mileage on the clock is correct, or if a new clock has been fitted.
- The Act put a stop to sharp practices on 'sale bargains'. A trader cannot claim that it is a lower 'sale' price unless the old price has been charged for at least 28 days during the previous six months.

Look out for labels

Here are some of the main labels you will see in shops, giving advice, information or warnings. More are coming into use all the time.

British Electrotechnical Approvals Board

Safety requirements have been laid down for the majority of domestic electrical appliances and the mark of the *British Electrotechnical Approvals Board* is your assurance that the product is safe.

British Standards Institution

The Kitemark appears on a wide range of products complying with standards laid down by the *British Standards Institution* – from car safety belts to pressure cookers.

The Safety Mark appears only on goods which comply with British Standards for safety. Examples are certain types of gas appliances and light fittings. Manufacturers wishing to use either mark must first submit their products to BSI for testing, and there are periodic tests of the goods and factory.

The BSI has a *Consumer Standards Advisory Committee* at 2 Park Street, London W1A 2BS.

Design Centre

Products with this label have been selected for the *Design Centre* as being well made, easy to use, suited to their purpose, simple to maintain, good looking and value for money. An illustrated index of well-designed consumer goods can be seen at the Design Centre, Haymarket, London SW1Y 4SU, and at The Scottish Design Centre, 72 St Vincent Street, Glasgow G2 5TN.

National Inspection Council for Electrical Installation Contracting

Your local Electricity Board shop has a list of reliable contractors in your area, who may display this label. These contractors are regularly inspected and approved by the *National Inspection Council for Electrical Installation Contracting*, an independent non-profit-making organisation set up for the protection of electricity consumers against faulty, unsafe, or otherwise defective electrical installations.

Home Laundering Consultative Council

A garment care label of the *Home Laundering Consultative Council* tells you exactly how to care for the garment to which it is attached, giving specific water temperatures and so on. A guide to the washing processes appears on all detergent packs, and washing machine instructions use the HLCC washing temperatures and terms.

	MACHINE	HAND WASH
4/50	Hand-hot medium wash	Hand-hot
	Cold rinse. Short spin or drip-dry	
△	DO NOT USE CHLORINE BLEACH	
⌐	WARM	
P	DRY CLEANABLE	
O	TUMBLE DRYING BENEFICIAL	

Furniture safety

Under the *Consumer Safety Act*, display labels must be attached to new upholstered furniture which is not resistant to lighted cigarettes, matches or (as illustrated here) both. Permanent labels must also be attached, warning of the dangers.

Standards

Other safeguards for the public are in recognised standards. For example, the weight of pre-packed food has to be clearly shown on a package and this must be the weight of the goods themselves, excluding the packaging (which often weighs more than the goods!). The standards of weights and measures are checked by inspectors from the Trading Standards departments, who have a right (by law) to visit any trader and check the goods on sale.

There are organisations, too, which check on goods. The British Standards Institution, for example, tests products and if they are up to the standard set by the BSI, they are given the 'kitemark' seal of approval.

Other standards are strictly laid down by law, such as those for paraffin heaters, crash helmets and car safety belts.

Another set of standards concerns advertising. The Broadcasting Act, 1981 requires independent television to exclude all advertising which may be likely to mislead the public. An organisation which sets strict controls in advertising is the Advertising Standards Authority. It has a code of good practice, covering all non-broadcast media such as newspapers, magazines, posters and the cinema. Here is an article which is placed in magazines and newspapers by the Authority.

DO ADVERTISEMENTS SOMETIMES DISTORT THE TRUTH?

The short answer is yes, some do. Every week hundreds of thousands of advertisements appear for the very first time.

Nearly all of them play fair with the people they are addressed to.

A handful do not. They misrepresent the products they are advertising.

As the Advertising Standards Authority it is our job to make sure these ads are identified, and stopped.

WHAT MAKES AN ADVERTISEMENT MISLEADING?

If a training course had turned a 7 stone weakling into Mr Universe the fact could be advertised because it can be proved.

But a promise to build 'you' into a 15 stone he-man would have us flexing our muscles because the promise could not always be kept.

'Makes you look younger' might be a reasonable claim for a cosmetic.

But pledging to 'take years off your life' would be an overclaim akin to a promise of eternal youth.

A garden centre's claim that its seedlings would produce 'a riot of colour in just a few days' might be quite contrary to the reality.

Such flowery prose would deserve to be pulled out by the roots.

If a brochure advertised a hotel as being '5 minutes walk to the beach,' it must not require an Olympic athlete to do it in the time.

As for estate agents, if the phrase 'overlooking the river' translated to 'backing onto a ditch,' there would be nothing for it but to show their ad the door.

HOW DO WE JUDGE THE ADS WE LOOK INTO?

Our yardstick is The British Code of Advertising Practice.

Its 500 rules give advertisers precise practical guidance on what they can and cannot say. The rules are also a gauge for media owners to assess the acceptability of any advertising they are asked to publish.

The Code covers magazines, newspapers, cinema commercials, brochures, leaflets, posters, circulars posted to you, and now commercials on video tapes.

The ASA is not responsible for TV and radio advertising. Though the rules are very similar they are administered by the Independent Broadcasting Authority.

WHY IT'S A TWO-WAY PROCESS

Unfortunately some advertisers are unaware of the Code, and breach the rules unwittingly. Others forget, bend or deliberately ignore the rules.

That is why we keep a continuous check on advertising. But because of the sheer volume, we cannot monitor every advertiser all the time.

So we encourage the public to help by telling us about any advertisements they think ought not to have appeared. Last year over 7,500 people wrote to us.

WHAT DO WE DO TO ADVERTISERS WHO DECEIVE THE PUBLIC?

Our first step is to ask advertisers who we or the public challenge to back up their claims with solid evidence.

If they cannot, or refuse to, we ask them either to amend the ads or withdraw them completely.

Nearly all agree without any further argument.

In any case we inform the publishers, who will not knowingly accept any ad which we have decided contravenes the Code.

If the advertiser refuses to withdraw the advertisement he will find it hard if not impossible to have it published.

WHOSE INTERESTS DO WE REALLY REFLECT?

The Advertising Standards Authority was not created by law and has no legal powers.

Not unnaturally some people are sceptical about its effectiveness.

In fact the Advertising Standards Authority was set up by the advertising business to make sure the system of self control worked in the public interest.

For this to be credible, the ASA has to be totally independent of the business.

Neither the chairman nor the majority of ASA council members are allowed to have any involvement in advertising.

Though administrative costs are met by a levy on the business, no advertiser has any influence over ASA decisions.

Advertisers are aware it is as much in their own interests as it is in the public's that honesty should be seen to prevail.

If you would like to know more about the ASA and the rules it seeks to enforce you can write to us at the address below for an abridged copy of the Code.

The Advertising Standards Authority.✓
If an advertisement is wrong, we're here to put it right.

ASA Ltd, Dept. T, Brook House, Torrington Place, London WC1E 7HN.

Assignments

1. Keep your eyes open for advertisements (particularly for aftershave, deodorants, cigarettes and chocolates) which suggest that if you use them you will be irresistible to the opposite sex. Make a list of the brand or trade names of the goods.

2. Make a list of goods which you see carrying the kitemark, the BEAB mark, and the Gas Council approval mark.

3. Packaging is a science and an art. It is scientific because of the skilful use of materials (such as plastics for longlife in freezers), and artistic because of the clever design which can often give the impression of real bulk, when inside there is only a very small bottle or a few sweets. Investigate the use of packag-

69

ing in these ways, and collect examples of them.

4 Having read the article by the Advertising Standards Authority, what are the examples quoted of 'misleading' statements in advertisements? Do you think this criticism is fair?

Which?

In 1957 the Consumers' Association was set up. It is a kind of 'watchdog' group which does valuable work in protecting people's interests. A monthly magazine, *Which?* contains information on the quality, reliability and safety of many products. It recommends 'value-for-money buys' and has been very critical of poor goods. *Which?* has been tremendously influential in raising standards, and manufacturers take careful notice of what the writers say about their own and their rivals' products. Specialist magazines are available now, such as **Motoring Which?**, **Money Which?** and **Holiday Which?**

In order to test products, the Consumers' Association buys them. No 'free gifts' are accepted from manufacturers and no free samples are taken, either.

Credit

The growth of credit has been enormous in recent years. 'Credit' means the consumer, instead of paying for the goods immediately by paying cash or signing a cheque, can pay over a period of time.

One way of doing this is by means of a *credit card*. This is issued by a bank, and it allows the holder to obtain goods immediately. You, the buyer, either settle the account with the bank at the end of the month, or put off payment to the bank for a month or two, paying interest on the loan to the bank through the credit card service – Access, Barclaycard etc. There are other credit card systems, such as American Express, where there is a payment to join, but afterwards the holder can negotiate good credit terms.

Another way of spreading payments over a long period is by *hire purchase* (HP). What happens is that a customer asks a shop if he or she can pay 'by HP'. The shop usually does not finance HP themselves (although the big multiple stores have their own credit systems) but usually they pass the HP request to a finance company. The customer pays a deposit to the shop. The finance company pays the shop the remainder of the purchase price. The customer pays the full cost in instalments to the finance company, plus, of course, the interest payments. Obviously, the consumer ends up paying more than the purchase price.

The Consumer Credit Act 1974

Parliament passed this law to provide good protection for the consumer. For example:

- There is a 'cooling-off' period for the consumer after signing a loan agreement which allows for a change of mind.
- Customers have the right to see any file kept on them by a credit reference agency, and can have mistakes corrected.

- Every consumer credit business has to be registered and obtain a licence from the Office of Fair Trading.

There are other parts to this Act, which together give the consumer a lot of protection from 'extortionate' credit financiers, that is, businesses which charge very high interest rates without making it clear to customers.

Assignments

1 What are the advantages of buying goods by credit? After you have listed them, make a second list of the disadvantages.
2 Mr Smith doesn't often go shopping. In a supermarket he can choose from three different sizes and three different prices:
   (a) The Washo carton is 900 g and costs 98p.
   (b) Suds is in a 1000 g pack and costs £1.06.
   (c) Dax is 800 g and costs 92p.

Which of the three packs is the best value for money? Suggest ways of overcoming this problem of different sizes and different prices.

3 A suite of furniture is on sale at a local store. Mr and Mrs Ahmed decide to buy. The sales assistant explains that there are three ways they can pay:
   (a) The cash price of £580.
   (b) On hire purchase, they can pay £100 deposit now and spread the rest over 12 monthly payments of £45.
   (c) On a longer term hire purchase, there is no deposit and they can spread the payments over 24 months at £32 a month.

Work out the difference in the total sums paid for the suite. Explain why goods cost more when they are bought on credit.

Goods which are bought on hire purchase do not belong to the purchaser until the last payment has been made. What could the store do if the purchaser fell behind with the payments?

People at work

21
The individual at work

Rights and duties

Every employee has rights at work. And they have duties, too. The same is true of employers: they have rights and responsibilities to their workforce. Some of these rights are defined by law, but others depend on the kind of job that people do, and the conditions and terms of their contract of employment. This chapter looks at some of these rights and duties.

Jobs for the boys – and the girls

Just over 56 million people live in Britain. Of these, 31 million are not employed. They are infants, children and students at school or college, parents who are at home, people who are too ill to work, the elderly, and potential workers who are on the unemployment register (about 3 million). This leaves Britain's *employed* total at just over 25 million, aged between 16 and 65 (although there are also employed workers who are over 65!).

Over the last 100 years, the range of jobs has changed dramatically. In 1885, most people worked in farming or in the mining and manufacturing industries. These were *labour intensive* which means that they needed large numbers of workers. But times have changed. With advances in technology, fewer people are needed in factories, on the land and for unskilled jobs. Service industries have grown, and today over 14 million people are employed in insurance, catering, transport, shops, education, central and local government, the Armed Services – these are the service industries. The rest of Britain's workforce are still within the primary and manufacturing industries.

Job selection
People are selected for jobs on the basis of:

- qualifications ✓
- knowledge ✓
- skills ✓
- experience ✓

For young people, going into a job for the first time, basic qualifications are very important. These give them the first foothold on the ladder of a career. Having made a start, training and experience can come later.

Job categories

One way of dividing jobs into different groups is according to the *level of qualifications and skills required*. This is how it is done by employment advisers:

Group 1: Professional and executive. These are the top jobs. The group includes professionals such as lawyers, doctors, teachers, pilots, vets, officers in the Armed Forces, senior scientists, directors, managers and senior civil servants. They are likely to have university degrees, professional qualifications and a lot of experience in local or central government, business or industry.

Group 2: Administrative jobs. They are managers and administrators, with high qualifications and plenty of experience, but perhaps without university degrees. They occupy senior jobs in government, shops and stores, business and industrial firms.

Group 3: Clerical and skilled staff. This is the largest group of people. The clerical section includes staff who work in offices, libraries, commerce and industry. The skilled workers have normally served a period of apprenticeship (which can last for up to 5 years) or training (up to 2 years) after leaving school. If they serve out their apprenticeship, they are recognised as skilled craftsmen or women who can practise their 'trade'. These include plumbers, carpenters, vehicle mechanics, electricians and so on.

Group 4: Semi-skilled. This kind of work requires some training, perhaps up to a year, but without the qualifications earned by a long apprenticeship. Machine operators in factories are in this group.

Group 5: Unskilled workers. This is a category of people whose jobs require only a little training of perhaps a few weeks. The work can be dirty or dangerous. It could involve 'unsocial hours' which means working at times when other people are at home. Examples are labourers, refuse collectors, working in a bar or serving in a café.

Group 6: Artists. These are people who have plenty of skills and undergo training but don't fit into any other category. They are actors, musicians, writers and artists, and also sport professionals such as footballers and snooker players.

These groups are not rigid. There is a lot of moving about between groups. For instance, someone who leaves school at 16 can train to be a skilled worker; then take additional qualifications at college in order to become a manager; and later add to his or her skills and experience in order to join Group 1 as a senior manager.

Training

Training is a very important part of any job. No one will get very far in their work without it. There are many ways of obtaining training. Here are some of them:

At school. A good, all-round education is a basic qualification. Passes at O-level (in 1988, GCSE), or O-grade in Scotland, are usually needed for office jobs and to obtain an apprenticeship. To go on to higher education, it is necessary to stay at school or college, taking A-level (or Scottish Higher grade) examinations.

Colleges. Further education colleges (sometimes called technical colleges or colleges of technology) offer courses leading to A-level for people who don't stay on at school. In addition, there are vocational courses (this means that the education is closely tied to a definite job) in subjects such as computing, engineering, catering, hairdressing, printing, art and design, secretarial and business studies, and many others. These courses can lead to a certificate or diploma awarded by the City & Guilds, or by the Business and Technician Education Council (BTEC).

Preparation for work. Many 16-year-olds now go straight on to a Youth Training Scheme (YTS) course. This involves real work experience and 'off-the-job' training at a college.

Training at work. Once people start work at 16, 17 or older, they are usually trained by their employer. This might mean finding out about the job from an experienced person, and it could take you only days or weeks to pick up the skill and knowledge. It could mean attending classes within the company, and, in addition, attending technical college for one or more days a week (called 'day release') for a year or more. Or, the employer might send the trainee to college for a month or longer on a 'block-release' scheme.

Higher education. People with good O-level and A-level results can go on to higher education. This involves attending a full-time course at a college, polytechnic or university to study for a diploma, a higher national diploma, or a degree. These are in all kinds of subjects from art to zoology. A feature of many courses is to provide students with work experience in companies as part of the course at college.

Try this

One way of describing training for jobs is to divide jobs into 11 'family groups'. The reason is that when people are trained for a task, they are given skills which apply within the whole

a.
- nurse
- home help
- dentist
- health visitor

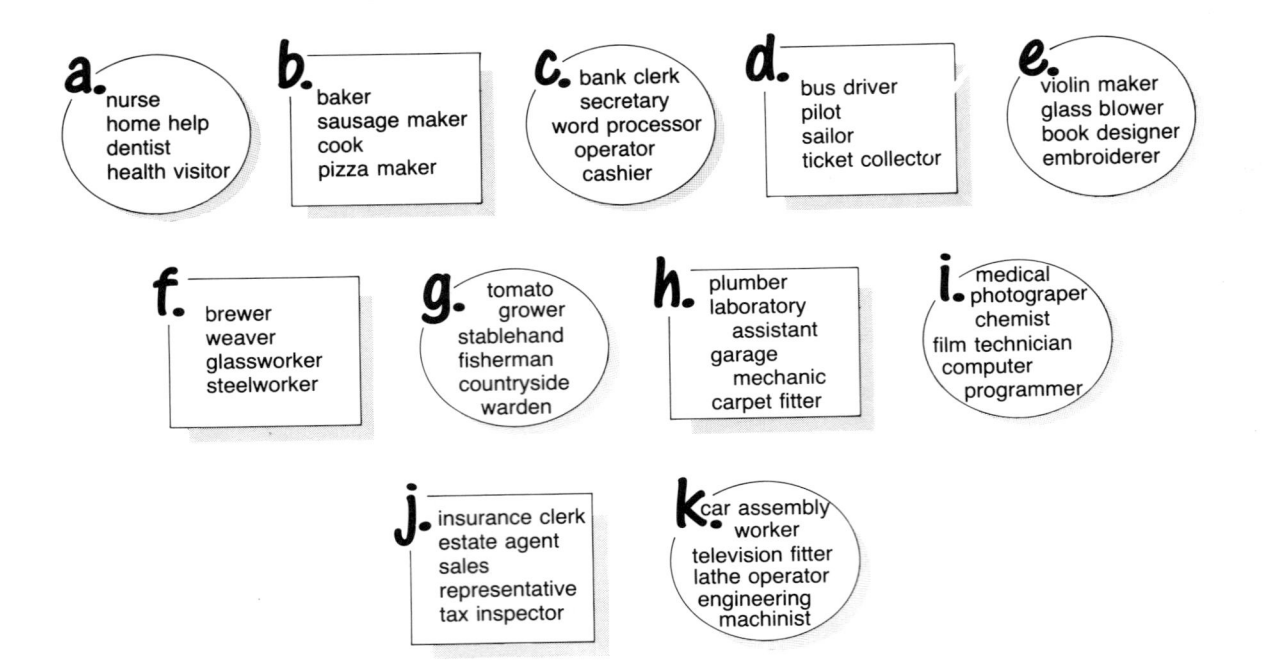

b.
- baker
- sausage maker
- cook
- pizza maker

c.
- bank clerk
- secretary
- word processor operator
- cashier

d.
- bus driver
- pilot
- sailor
- ticket collector

e.
- violin maker
- glass blower
- book designer
- embroiderer

f.
- brewer
- weaver
- glassworker
- steelworker

g.
- tomato grower
- stablehand
- fisherman
- countryside warden

h.
- plumber
- laboratory assistant
- garage mechanic
- carpet fitter

i.
- medical photograper
- chemist
- film technician
- computer programmer

j.
- insurance clerk
- estate agent
- sales representative
- tax inspector

k.
- car assembly worker
- television fitter
- lathe operator
- engineering machinist

'family'. Here is the 11-family grouping:
1. Administrative, clerical and office services.
2. Agriculture, horticulture, forestry and fishing.
3. Craft and design.
4. Installation, maintenance and repair.
5. Technical and scientific.
6. Manufacturing and assembly.
7. Processing with machinery.
8. Food preparation and services.
9. Personal service and sales.
10. Community and health services.
11. Transport services.

Above are 11 sets of jobs. What you have to do is to match them up with the families listed above. The answers are at the bottom of the page.

Employment and the law

When you are offered and accept a job, a contract is made. The terms of the contract don't have to be written down. The information which you are given at an interview counts just as much as a piece of paper. However, no later than 13 weeks after starting work, an employee must be given a *written contract of employment*. This contains details about:
- the date of starting work.
- the name of the company.
- the hours of work and agreed holidays.
- the rate of pay and whether payment is weekly or monthly.
- overtime rates.
- the time of starting and leaving.

Having a job also involves *duties* as well as rights. An employer expects people to work to the best of their ability, to be punctual, honest, careful and loyal. Dishonesty (such as stealing the company's goods), lateness, working too slowly or carelessly can lead to dismissal.

Training isn't a right, either. But if the written statement says training will be given, the employee has a right to it. (To make sure, the employee should try to persuade the employer to include training in the contract of employment.)

Pay

The law says that every employee is entitled to a pay statement. This shows the total amount of wages before anything is taken off, and the deductions such as tax and national insurance. (National insurance contributions are payments by both employer and employee towards the cost of health services.) A pay slip or pay state-

Answers
A10, B8, C1, D11, E3, F7, G2, H4, J5, K9, L6.

74

ment contains other information, too, such as union dues (payments to the union), and deductions towards a company's pension or sickness schemes. Here is a typical pay advice statement.

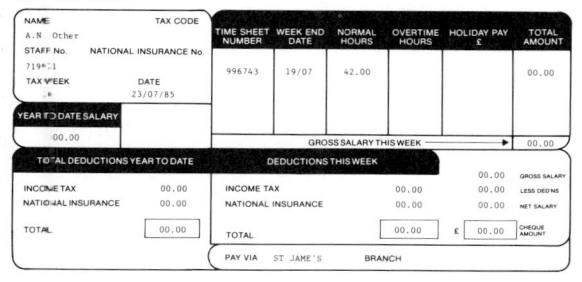

Being off sick
If someone is ill and cannot get to work, they should phone their employer or try to get someone to deliver a message. From April 1986 a new government scheme of sick pay came into operation. It is called SSP (Statutory Sick Pay). It makes employers responsible for paying sick pay (SSP) to employees for up to twenty-eight weeks of sickness absence in one year. Trainees on YTS don't come under SSP, nor do people who are in their first three months of employment.

Health and Safety
Parliament passed a new Act in 1974 which set out the duties of employers and employees on health and safety. Companies are responsible for protecting employees against risks to health and safety. Among the duties of employers are these:
- to maintain a safe and healthy place to work.
- to ensure a safe exit and entry to premises.
- to maintain safety from dangerous substances such as explosives and poisons.
- to maintain safe machinery and equipment.
- to use safe methods of handling and transporting materials.
- to train all employees in health and safety.

To make sure that employers are operating within the Act, government inspectors can go into factories, shops and colleges to check on machinery and safety standards.

Employees have duties, too. Under the act of parliament, they must:
- act sensibly with care for others as well as themselves.
- make sure all the company's safety measures are carried out.

If someone does have an accident at work, they can claim *compensation*. But not if it was their fault. Within 28 days of an accident, an employee can claim industrial injury benefit.

Dismissal and redundancy
People can't be sacked from a job at a moment's notice, without reason and without pay. The law protects workers from instant dismissal except for stealing and other crimes. The law states that any employee who has worked continuously for at least six months and who is then paid off can ask for a written statement of the reasons for dismissal. An employee who has worked for four weeks must give at least one week's notice.

Another set of rights concerns dismissal for inadequate work. If an employer is thinking of dismissing someone because of poor work, they must:
- give a warning about the employee's work.
- give adequate notice, if the warnings are ignored.
- provide a written statement of reasons for dismissal.

Redundancy is a polite way of being dismissed or 'given the sack'. The result is the same – someone loses their job. Redundancy is usually caused by a company's collapse or loss of business, so that employees have to be paid off. Or it could be that the company moves its production to another part of the country. The law says that if a person is made redundant, the employer has to:
- try to find ways of avoiding the closure of business.
- tell the trade unions about the situation.
- give employees sufficient notice of the pay-offs.
- pay all money owing to employees, plus holiday pay entitlement.

If employees have worked for the company for more than two years since they were 18, they qualify for extra payments. The amount paid to them (often called the 'lump sum') depends of the age, length of service and wage of the employee.

Equal opportunities
The law also says that women must be treated equally when they apply for a job and when they are at work. Under the Sex Discrimination Act, 1975, it is against the law for employers to discriminate on the grounds of sex, or against married people. Under the Equal Pay Act, 1970, women can claim equal pay if the job they do is the same work or broadly similar to work done by a man.

It is also against the law to treat people differently because of race. The Race Relations Act, 1976 says that employers must not discriminate on the grounds of race, colour, or nationality. This means when people apply for a job and at work.

Complaints about race or sex discrimination are heard by industrial tribunals. The Equal Opportunities Commission (EOC) and the Commission for Racial Equality (CRE) can both be asked to help. In addition, trade unions will come to the support of members who feel they are being unfairly treated by employers.

Making a complaint
Let's suppose that a young worker or trainee in a company thinks that they should complain about the way a company has treated them. What happens?

The first thing to do is to raise the matter with their supervisor or the manager. In most cases this will lead to some kind of action. But if the employee still isn't satisfied? The next stop should be the shop steward of the trade union, assuming that the worker belongs to a union. What if that doesn't work, or there isn't a union? In 1974 an organisation called ACAS, the Advisory, Conciliation and Arbitration Service, was set up. There is a head office in London and regional offices around the country. Its job is to provide advice on industrial relations. It has the power to make inquiries and to ask employers questions. ACAS may advise an appeal to an *industrial tribunal*. This is like a law court but is much easier to understand.

Each tribunal is made up of a lawyer and two other people who know about industry. They deal with complaints about:
- redundancy
- maternity leave
- pay
- unfair dismissal
- race and sex discrimination

A tribunal can order an employer to act fairly which means to give a person his or her job back, or pay compensation.

There are other rights and issues concerning work such as the right to pregnancy and maternity leave, time off for public duties, the rights of disabled or handicapped people, pension scheme rights, the powers of the police and security guards at workplaces, industrial action and picketing. If you are interested in these topics and want to know more about them, you should read *Your Rights at Work* by Bill Birtles and Patricia Hewitt, published by the National Council for Civil Liberties.

What's your attitude?
On the facing page you will find three cases involving rights. What do you think of the views in these examples?

Questions

In your notebook, write a few lines about each of these:
(a) a contract of employment.
(b) a pay advice slip.
(c) health and safety at work.
(d) an employee's duties at work.
(e) equal opportunities at work.

MEN SHOULD BE PAID A LOT MORE BECAUSE THEY WORK HARDER THAN WOMEN
WOMEN ARE MUCH CLEVERER SO THEY SHOULD BE PAID MORE THAN MEN
I'VE COME ABOUT THE JOB OF TECHNICIAN WHICH IS ADVERTISED
SORRY BUT THE JOB'S FOR A MAN. WOMEN LEAVE TO HAVE BABIES...
HELLO! I'M KIRPAL MANJI. I HEAR THERE'S A JOB AS A CANTEEN MANAGER IS IT STILL VACANT?
SORRY, BUT THE JOB'S NO LONGER AVAILABLE

22
Labour relations

Timsons Engineering

When Jack Johnson walked through the entrance of Timsons as the new managing director, there were 14 employees.

'On my first day, I put on a pair of overalls and helped to finish a batch of overdue parts for an angry car manufacturer,' he said. 'On my second day, we lost a valuable overseas contract. At the end of the first week, two of the office staff walked out, saying they'd had enough of Timsons, thank you!'

Jack's task was to rebuild a firm damaged by lack of orders and bad management. Everyone feared that the company would collapse before Jack could get to work. The 12 survivors told him they would postpone pay rises, and if necessary they would work overtime without pay in order to get things moving again. Everyone at Timsons was a member of a trade union, and Jack Johnson belonged to an employers' organisation, the Engineering Employers' Federation (EEF). 'But we all agreed. None of these organisations or unions could help us a lot. If Timsons was to survive, it would be by our own efforts.'

Even so, in those dark days, one of the unions made an important contribution. Jack needed two skilled electrical workers. The local Branch secretary of the EETPU – the Electrical, Electronic, Telecommunication and Plumbing Union – kept a register of members looking for work, and within a week Jack had his two electricians. In the same week, he telephoned a director of another engineering company, who he'd met at an employers' conference organised by EEF, and this quickly led to a fresh contract for Timsons with a manufacturer looking for precision-made machine tools. Within three years, the company was on the mend. The workforce grew to 42, production had increased, and the threat of closure was a bad memory.

Take-over

Then came a different kind of bombshell.

'I was sitting at my desk. The telephone rang, and the owners of Timsons told me that we'd been sold.'

The new owners were International Technology, a very large organisation with a workforce of 41 000 people in 70 factories spread over Europe.

At first, little changed. Jack Johnson continued as managing director, although he was visited regularly by finance, sales and production staff from 'Big Brother'.

'Then, after one of these visits, the telephone rang again. I was told that it had been decided that Timsons would now concentrate on one product only, a steering column assembly unit, which would be supplied to one customer, a major car manufacturer.'

The union representatives, the staff and Jack had worries about concentrating all their business with one manufacturer, but they agreed, for wages went up and more production workers were taken on.

For the next two years, Timsons did very well indeed. Then came 'bombshell number three'.

'I could see it coming. It was no surprise. The car manufacturer was building new models. We put in designs for the steering assembly packs, but at the last minute the manufacturer switched the business to another supplier.'

Timsons, having lost 90 per cent of its business overnight, continued for two months, and was then closed down. The last, sad task of the unions was to negotiate redundancy payments for the staff. Jack Johnson moved on to be manager at another factory within International Technology where he used his contacts, skills and knowledge for the benefit of the organisation.

Trade unions

This sad tale, which is based on a real company, is not unusual in the engineering industry. Within the story are clues to the value of having trade unions and employers' organisations. In this chapter we shall look at the reasons and benefits of belonging to these groups.

When Timsons had only 12 workers, they all knew Jack Johnson personally. Negotiations over wages, hours and conditions of work were all conducted face-to-face. But once Timsons were drawn into International Technology, and the workforce grew, relations between managers and workers became more complicated. The staff now felt they needed to ask for the help and strength of the trade unions.

What is a trade union?
A trade union is formed by a group of people doing the same job, or with the same skills, or who work in the same industry. By combining together in the interests of the members, the union aims to get the best pay and working conditions that can be negotiated from employers.

Trade unions get their power from their members. Regular contributions are paid by members as a percentage of their wages, and by saving and banking, the union can build up a solid basis to provide benefits for members and to pay the salaries of full-time officials. The average weekly contribution is about 47p.

Power also comes from the *number* of members. The Transport and General Workers Union has over 1½ million members. By combining together, the members, led by their elected leaders, negotiate from a position of strength. Most employers prefer to deal with a union. If they did not, they would have to cope with wage claims and all kinds of requests from hundreds of different sections and departments, or separately from thousands of workers.

Members of the matchmakers union in 1888

From Tolpuddle to today
For hundreds of years, trade unions were forbidden by Acts of Parliament. Anyone who formed a union to raise wages or to reduce the hours of work was sent to prison. About 150 years ago the law was changed so that workers had a little more freedom. In 1829 the Agricultural Workers' Union was created. A few years later, six farm labourers of Tolpuddle, in Dorset, protested about the reduction of wages and technically broke the law. In March 1834 the men were sentenced to seven years' deportation to Australia, having been found guilty of taking 'unlawful oaths' (although they were later pardoned and brought back to Britain). The 'Tolpuddle Martyrs' as they were called, became a symbol of oppression. The fight went on to obtain freedom to form workers' associations. In 1851 the Amalgamated Society of Engineers was set up and became a model for unions representing skilled workers.

The next milestone in trade union history occured in 1868 when the Trades Union Congress met for the first time. This was a meeting of separate unions, and they agreed to cooperate together, electing a General Secretary and other officials to represent them.

The next breakthrough came in 1871 when it was agreed that membership of a union was not against the law. From then on, the machinery of negotiating with employers was created, and many trade unions backed the new Labour Party, formed in the early years of the 20th century.

After the 1914–18 war, unemployment rose and in 1926 there was a general strike which began when mineworkers protested at cuts in their wages. The strike lasted only nine days and ended in great bitterness.

After the Second World War, the unions increased their membership and their power, and there were many conflicts with employers and governments. Several new Acts of Parliament, called Labour Relations Acts, were passed in the 1970s. These extended the rights of unions and their members and allowed the formation of 'closed shops'. This is an agreement between an employer and one or more trade unions that certain employees are required to be members of the union in order to hold the job.

The most recent laws, the Employment Acts

of 1980 and 1982, defined employees' rights. Among these rights are:

Written terms of employment. As soon as a job is offered and accepted, there is a contract and the employer has to give the employee written details of the main terms and conditions of employment.

Trade union membership. Every employee has the right to become a member of a trade union, and can take part in the activities of the union.

Time off. Officials of unions have the right to time off work to carry out their duties.

Maternity rights. Female workers are entitled to maternity pay from their employer and have the right to return to work.

The Employment Act, 1982 requires companies with more than 250 employees to explain what they have done to improve employee participation. The Act also extended the use of secret ballots to test support for closed shops and strikes. This Act altered the wording of a 'trade dispute' so that to be 'lawful', a dispute must be between workers and their own employer.

Over the last 150 years, many Acts of Parliament have been passed to deal with trade unions, labour relations, strikes, disputes and conditions of employment. This shows how difficult it is to decide on the best form of law. And laws don't stop trade unions from protesting when they believe the interests of their members are threatened, as we saw in 1984 during the miners' strike. In the end, an agreement has to be reached so that employers and employees can work together for their common good.

What do unions do?

Over ten million people belong to trade unions because of the benefits which they receive. Here is a list of some of things that unions work for:
- improved wages.
- shorter working week.
- help for the unemployed.
- equal opportunities.
- longer holidays.
- education and training.
- a share in the planning and control of industry.
- improved health and safety.
- better conditions at work, such as heating, lighting, ventilation.
- job satisfaction and prospects.

When men and women join a union, they get a book of rules and a list of the benefits provided by the union for its members.

Types of unions

There are four main kinds of trade unions.

1 *Craft unions*
They represent skilled workers who have been trained in practical and technical skills. Among them are engineers, electricians, plumbers, printers and others.

2 *General unions*
They represent unskilled or semi-skilled workers, working in many different industries. A union of this type is the TGWU – the Transport and General Workers' Union.

3 *Industrial unions*
They represent workers in one industry such as the NUM (National Union of Miners), NALGO (National Association of Local Government Officers), and the NUR. What does NUR stand for?

4 *Professional unions*
They represent clerical workers, civil servants, supervisors, teachers. Among them is the AUT (Association of University Teachers), and the NUJ (National Union of Journalists). This is the expanding sector of unionism, with 4.3 million men and women, or 30% of the total membership of trade unions.

Trade union organisation

The shop steward

When people start work for the first time, the union member they are likely to meet first is the shop steward. Union members at any workplace elect their own spokesperson, and this is the shop steward or union representative. It is an unpaid job, for a shop steward carries on with the normal job but is allowed some time off for union duties. The steward deals with problems in the factory or office, and is an important link in communications between the staff and managers.

Branch secretary

Union members belong to a local branch which meets regularly to discuss union business. Each branch has a secretary (usually a full-time official), a chairperson and a committee. They send delegates to the union's annual national conference, where policy is decided on.

Head office

Each union has a national committee, made up of elected delegates from the branches. Most unions have full-time paid officials who advise shop stewards, visit branches and assist the work of the Trades Union Congress.

Trades Union Congress

The TUC is a voluntary association of trade unions. Delegates from the member unions meet at a conference each year to consider matters which affect them. The Congress has met every year since 1871 (except for the first year, 1914, of the Great War). The total number of unions within the TUC is 98, with a total membership of over 10 million members affiliated to the TUC.

The General Council of the TUC is elected: it keeps a close eye on all industrial developments and presses governments about unemployment and other concerns. There is a permanent office of the TUC in London, with a staff led by the General Secretary.

The organisation of trade unions is like this:

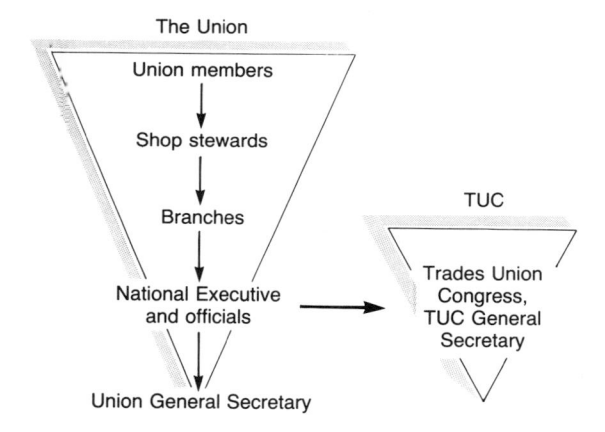

```
The Union
  Union members
       ↓
  Shop stewards
       ↓
  Branches                    TUC
       ↓
  National Executive     Trades Union
  and officials    →     Congress,
       ↓                 TUC General
                         Secretary
  Union General Secretary
```

How it works

In the factory or offices

When you start your first job, it is likely that you'll soon be approached by a shop steward. You'll be asked if you would like to join the union. In some jobs, where there's a closed shop, you might have to join the union in order to have the job. The shop steward is elected by the workers each year. He/she looks after the interests of the members and helps to solve any problems they may have in the factory or offices.

Much of the work of a shop steward is in solving day-to-day problems. There may be a quarrel between two workers, or with a foreman. There may be a dispute between people of two different unions. At the Ford Motor Company works, at Dagenham in Essex, there are 16 different unions, and the management has to negotiate with all of them.

In a large factory such as the Ford works, there may be many shop stewards, working in different departments. They elect a leader called a *convenor* who arranges meetings for all the stewards from one union. At Ford, therefore, there could be 16 convenors.

In the branch office

The structure and working day of a local branch office varies between different unions. Usually, however, members of a union in the local area will meet for a branch or 'Lodge' meeting. They elect members to represent them on the district committee. Sometimes the local office has a permanent headquarters and full-time staff including the branch secretary.

Each year the local lodge or branch elects delegates to the national committee. This is likely to have full-time officials, including the President, the Secretary and office staff. The national committee is the most powerful body in the union, for it decides on day-to-day policy and it contains the most powerful people in the union.

In the TUC

The national committee elects delegates to the General Council of the TUC, and the local branch also elects representatives to district meetings of all trade unions. These are usually called Trade Councils, and bring together men and women from many unions.

Trade disputes

News of strikes regularly gets into the newspapers, and they are reported on radio and television. You'll often hear talk of strikes (or 'industrial disputes') when you start work.

The facts show that Britain has a good record of avoiding strikes. Over one year, for every one factory or workplace that has a strike, there are 19 other places that have no strikes or stoppages. Another interesting fact is that for every day 'lost' through strikes, there are 40 days lost through sickness or accidents.

Unions don't start strikes unless they feel they are forced into it, that is, when all negotiations have broken down. Unions, like managers, try to solve their differences peacefully. But if they think that nothing will come out of negotiation except delay, they may take an industrial dispute to a strike.

You may think that all strikes take place over pay. But that is only one cause. Other causes are

Miners Rally at Hyde Park before marching through London, February 1985

payoffs (when a company is reducing the size of the workforce); how many workers will be needed to operate a new machine; *victimisation* (this is when a worker feels he or she has been singled out unfairly); and the closure of factories. The miners' strike of 1984 began because of the policy of the National Coal Board to close pits which they classified as unprofitable.

In many factories there is a 'disputes procedure' committee which looks into the cause of unrest as soon as it happens. The union representatives and the managers try to find a solution, but if there is no agreement, the next step may be a strike.

Problems at Young's: a case-study

At Young's Ltd, all the work of making small wooden bathroom cabinets is done by workers who belong to a craft union.

The fitting of glass shelves is done by members of a general union who are paid less than the craftsmen. The management decide that the workers in the general union should also do the heat-sealing in plastic coverings and other packaging jobs.

Discuss

1 Young's Ltd soon had a serious industrial dispute on its hands, with two unions and the management at loggerheads. The dispute is about *'differentials'*, which is the difference in pay and conditions between one union and another.
What action do you think could be taken by the management and the unions to solve this dispute?
2 Do you think that doctors, nurses and emergency services should ever go on strike?
3 When a trade union negotiates a rise in pay, everyone in the factory gets the rise, even though some workers are not members of the union. Is this fair? Should the union insist on a closed shop, with everyone, all the production workers belonging to the union?

"WE DEMAND ADDITIONAL PAY FOR THIS WORK. WE AGREE THAT THE JOB ISN'T AS SKILLED AS CABINET MAKING BUT THE PACKAGERS NOW HAVE TO LEARN NEW SKILLS ON HEAT-SEALING MACHINES AND TO COMPENSATE FOR THIS WE SHOULD HAVE A PAY RISE."

"IF THE PACKAGERS GET A RISE SO SHOULD WE. WE HAVE TO SHOW THAT SKILLED WORKERS HAVE A RIGHT TO HIGHER RATES OF PAY. IF WE AREN'T CAREFUL THE MANAGEMENT WILL BE EMPLOYING UNSKILLED WORKERS IN SKILLED JOBS"

"WE ARE PREPARED TO GIVE THE GENERAL UNION PEOPLE A RISE IN WAGES BECAUSE THEY ARE BEING ASKED TO TAKE ON NEW TASKS, BUT WE HAVE NO INTENTION WHATSOEVER OF INCREASING THE PAY OF ANY OTHER WORKER IN THE FACTORY"

23
Employers' associations

Employers and managers can obtain help and advice from many different organisations. There is likely to be some kind of federation or association of firms in the same business. Among them are the Retail Consortium of companies involved in shops and stores, the Engineering Employers Association and the British Printing Industries Federation. There are over 200 of these *trade associations*.

These associations provide a meeting place for managers to share common problems. They organise conferences and courses, and they provide services such as marketing advice, insurance, safety and many other things, including some training services.

In most industries, too, the employers' association takes the lead or plays the major part in wage negotiations. There is often a *Joint National Council* which consists of representatives from the trade union national or executive committees, and representatives from the employers' side. The Council negotiates a wage agreement for the whole industry and thus lessens arguments at the factory level, although these still occur.

The CBI

Most of these associations are members of the *Confederation of British Industry* (CBI). The CBI was set up in 1965. It is an independent association of companies and organisations, financed entirely by industry and commerce.

Its objectives are to promote the interests of industry and to make sure that governments and people as a whole understand the needs, problems and plans of British business, and the contribution it makes to the prosperity of the country.

The CBI is generally recognised as the main

A meeting at the CBI conference

mouthpiece for business, and it is generally consulted by governments.

The CBI represents the management side of business and its views are generally those of very senior people – directors and managers. It also provides essential information and research services on behalf of its members. For instance, from time to time, the CBI puts out reports on economic surveys or bulletins on the state of industry and its views on what the government should or shouldn't be doing.

Membership of the CBI consists of more than 10 000 companies and over 200 trade associations and employers' organisations, in all representing over 12 million employees. Most of the nationalised industries are members.

The governing body of the CBI is the Council which meets monthly in London. It is assisted by about 30 committees which advise on the main aspects of policy. Then there are the 13 regional offices which are in contact with local authorities, MPs, businesses and individuals. Close contact is maintained with the TUC. Although the CBI and the TUC may at times have different policies, they both have the same ultimate goal which is to create more business, on which the prosperity of everyone depends.

The CBI also keeps in close touch with Ministers of the government, both through day-to-day contacts and as members of the National Economic Development Council (usually known as 'Neddy') which discusses economic policy. To find out more about the CBI, write for leaflets from CBI, 103 New Oxford Street, London WC1A 1DU.

The Institute of Directors

This is another national, London-based organisation. As its name suggests, it represents the top tier of industry and commerce, the directors. Like the CBI, it conducts surveys of members' opinions on the state of the British economy, prospects for exporters, and so on, and it tries to influence the government, newspapers and the media, and the general public on what the Institute thinks should be done to help British business.

Chambers of Commerce

So far, we have described employers' organisations at the national level, most of which have their headquarters in London. But there are also local and district organisations. Many of the national associations, such as the British Institute of Management and the CBI have local offices and activities. Then there are local committees of the trade associations: this means that motor trade suppliers (garages), retailers (shops), estate agents, caterers, and so on, have their own local groups.

There is also likely to be a local Chamber of Commerce. This is a meeting place for employers and managers from many different industries and businesses. Here the garage managers, fish shop owners, chemists, newsagents and other business people can meet to share their opinions and to ask for advice.

Test your knowledge

1. Find out the names or titles of five employers' associations which operate at a national level.
2. (a) Who belongs to the CBI?
   (b) Who does the CBI want to influence?
   (c) What services to its members is provided by the CBI?

24
Employee participation

An important development in recent years within industry has been 'employee participation'. This means that employees as well as owners and managers take a full part in the business or organisation.

Aims

The reasons for setting up a scheme of employee participation are as follows.
1 *Commitment and effort*
   The future success of industry depends on people's *commitment* to their work. Experience has shown that people put far more *effort* to make things work if they have taken part in the decision-making.
2 *Involvement and enjoyment*
   It has also been found out that if people are personally *involved*, they are more likely to *enjoy* their work.
3 *Satisfaction and results*
   When people are closely involved in helping the organisation to meet its objectives, their satisfaction generally leads to an improvement in their own knowledge, skills and attitudes to their job and to other people.

How to participate

The ways by which participation can work are as follows.
1 *By direct involvement*
   This includes improving the standard of work produced; suggesting new ways of doing things; improving working conditions.
2 *By information*
   Employees cannot be involved in *every* decision. But they can be brought into some of the really important decisions, such as moving to new premises, taking on extra work, staff changes, improving the system of work-flow, and so on. To make sure that employees have sufficient information to help them make decisions, there has to be two-way communication – from managers to workers, and in the other direction.

   Two-way communication can be achieved by several different methods. Here are some of them.
   - a company magazine or news-sheet.
   - a printed company report, specially for employees.
   - noticeboards in the offices and workshops.
   - regular meetings between managers and

Employee participation. The right approval . . .

. . . and the wrong approval

employee representatives.
- discussion groups.

Can you think of any others?

3 *By consultation*

To make sure that everyone with a view can be heard, the organisation needs to set up ways by which employees can be consulted, so their views are known before a final decision is taken.

In a big company, consultation is usually organised inside departments. One method is called a 'quality circle'. The circle is a group of managers and other staff. Together, they discuss, decide and act on ideas for improving the methods of doing things in the company. This is where trade unions come in, too. The union officials would expect to be consulted on important topics, so they can explain to the management the views of their members.

4 *By negotiation*

Negotiation can take place on many topics. Among them are likely to be working conditions, hours, pay, health and safety, and other things. Most negotiations are peacefully arranged and reach a conclusion that is satisfactory for both sides – management and employees. It is the negotiations which *don't* reach agreement that get into the news. When this happens, and *conflict* replaces *consultation*, it is defeat for participation.

How does participation work?

For the idea to be really effective, participation needs to take account of these factors.

1 *Consultation at work*

This is when the idea works best for most employees. People have a say in how their work is organised and done, how conditions might be improved, and how time and effort could be saved if things were done differently.

2 *Good communication*

This means making sure that employees are kept well informed on a regular basis about the company's business and where it is going in the future.

3 *Talking to the management*

If employees are going to assist in decision-taking, they have to be told the facts. This means asking the staff for their views at a very early stage and taking notice of these views.

Squaring the circle: a case-study

This is an example of a 'quality circle' at work. It is based on a real company which specialises in high-quality garments, produced in a non-stop stream. Read the account of the company's problems and suggest what the quality circle might do. Remember that the circle is made up of senior managers, supervisors, office staff, designers and machine operatives.

The main problem is time or lack of it. Everything has to be done at speed to increase the number of garments made per hour so that prices are kept down at a time when the company is being severely tested by competition from overseas, particularly Hong Kong. The methods of making the garments therefore have to be speeded up, but this is sacrificing quality.

There are four main groups of people who work for the company. The diagram shows who they are:
- *machine operatives* – who make the stockings, tights, and children's clothes from designs planned and drawn by designers.
- *designers* – who work in a studio at one end of the main building.
- *managers and office staff* – accounts department; order, sales and marketing sections; 'line' supervisors.
- *mechanics* – who maintain and repair machines and equipment.

clothes they have designed, but can't get time on them because of the need for constant production.
3 Inaccurate cutting of materials leads to waste. Sometimes, garments have to be scrapped because of errors in cutting. One of the main reasons for this is because new fabrics are sometimes introduced without time to test them properly.

And the solutions . . .?
If you were a member of the quality circle, what would you suggest? Write down your solutions – or suggestions for improvement – for the three problems.

This is what the company's quality circle suggested.

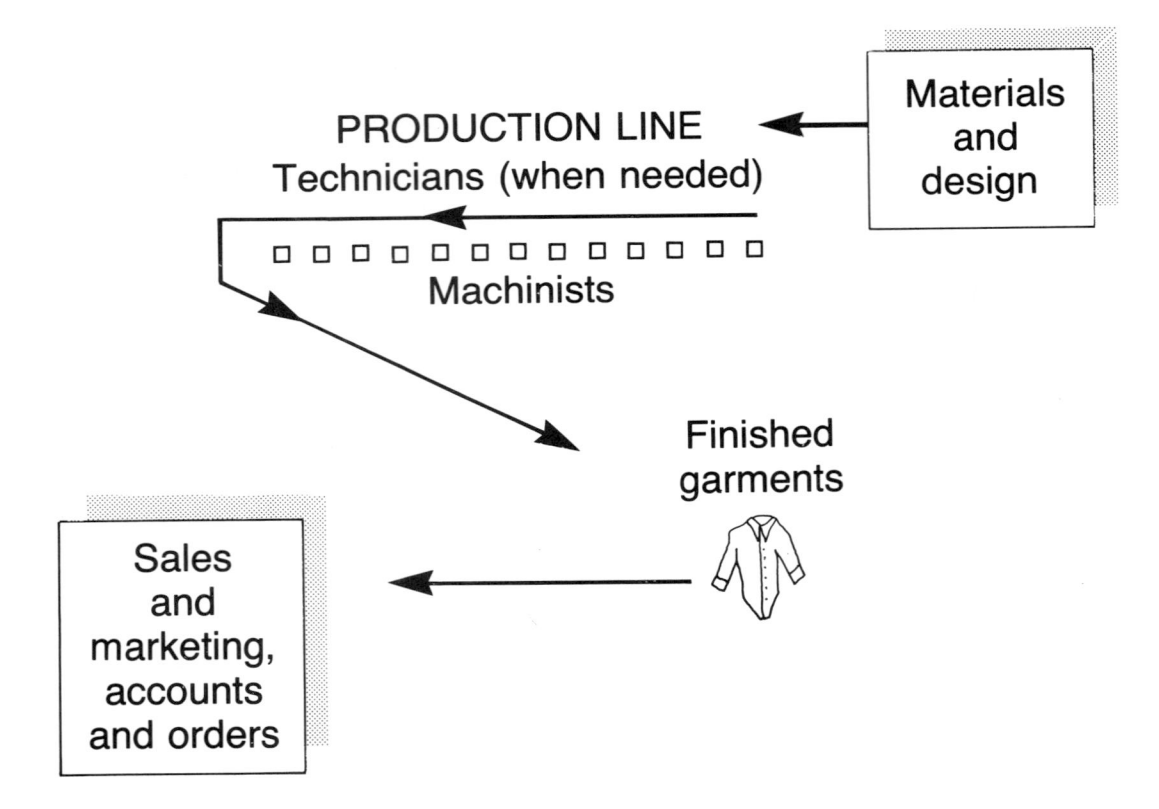

PRODUCTION LINE
Technicians (when needed)

Machinists

Materials and design

Finished garments

Sales and marketing, accounts and orders

The problems
1 When machines break down, the mechanics aren't sure which ones have priority, and often have to leave one job to repair an essential, but wonky, machine.
2 The designers complain that they need access to the machines in order to make the

1 The mechanics suggested a notice-board which they called *Ernie's Emergencies* (Ernie was the Works Manager).
Each day, the line managers wrote on the board which machines had to be attended to, in order of priority.
One mechanic, now given the name

'Speedy', could be called on *at any time*.
2 Two machines were bought and installed in the design section.
3 The machine operatives suggested a scheme by which there should be a miniature trial of new fabrics before they were used in production.

Did you have any other ideas?

Two-way communication

If the staff of a company are to be closely involved in decisions about the company's business, they have to be told about what is going on. As we have seen, communication of information and ideas should be two-way, like this:

'Passing the word'

There are many ways of communicating. In a small company, with perhaps 30 to 100 employees, the most effective method may be in 'passing the word'. This means that the managers and supervisors see people individually, or talk to small groups of people. This *face-to-face* method of explaining things is by far the most effective way because it allows the staff to respond, by asking questions and making their own viewpoints known.

In a bigger company, it is still possible to arrange face-to-face meetings, but it is likely that hundreds of people, rather than a dozen, will attend these 'teach-ins' organised by management.

Communication can also be made in writing. This would include notices, letters to staff, and reports.

Some companies use modern methods of communication such as loudspeakers (this can bring the accusation from staff that 'it's like being in a prison camp'), video, and closed circuit television.

Whatever method is used, the words need to carry messages about the company's policies and objectives; its financial position; the way that profits have been used; and benefits for employees.

For information to move *upwards*, that is from the staff to the managers, the same methods can be used. But the problem here is that the managers tend to organise the means of communication – *they* call a meeting, *they* send out reports and letters. This is why trade unions prefer a method where the workforce elects representatives to discuss policy with the managers. In this situation, the unions feel they can properly explain the feelings and opinions of the staff.

Let's look in some detail at one method of communication used by companies to communicate with customers and with their own staff – Annual Reports and Employee Reports.

The Annual Report

The main source of information about a company is the Annual Report. This is published to inform shareholders, customers and investors about the company. The Report also carries the financial details of the firm's business over the financial year.

Most companies take a great deal of trouble with their Annual Report. The objective is to present a picture of a successful business. However, if the company has suffered a bad year, this cannot be disguised. The financial facts and figures will show successes and failures.

Some companies publish two Annual Reports. One is for the general public. The other is for employees. In this, the firm tries to explain, in fairly simple terms, its objectives and financial standing. In this way, the two documents contribute to the process of communication.

Employee Reports

Reed International is a huge organisation which includes many separate businesses, ranging from a company with only 14 employees to another with 4000 people in 15 factories.

Among the products made by Reed are paper, packaging, paint, do-it-yourself products, magazines, books, newspapers. Among famous pro-

Where our total income of £2,115m goes

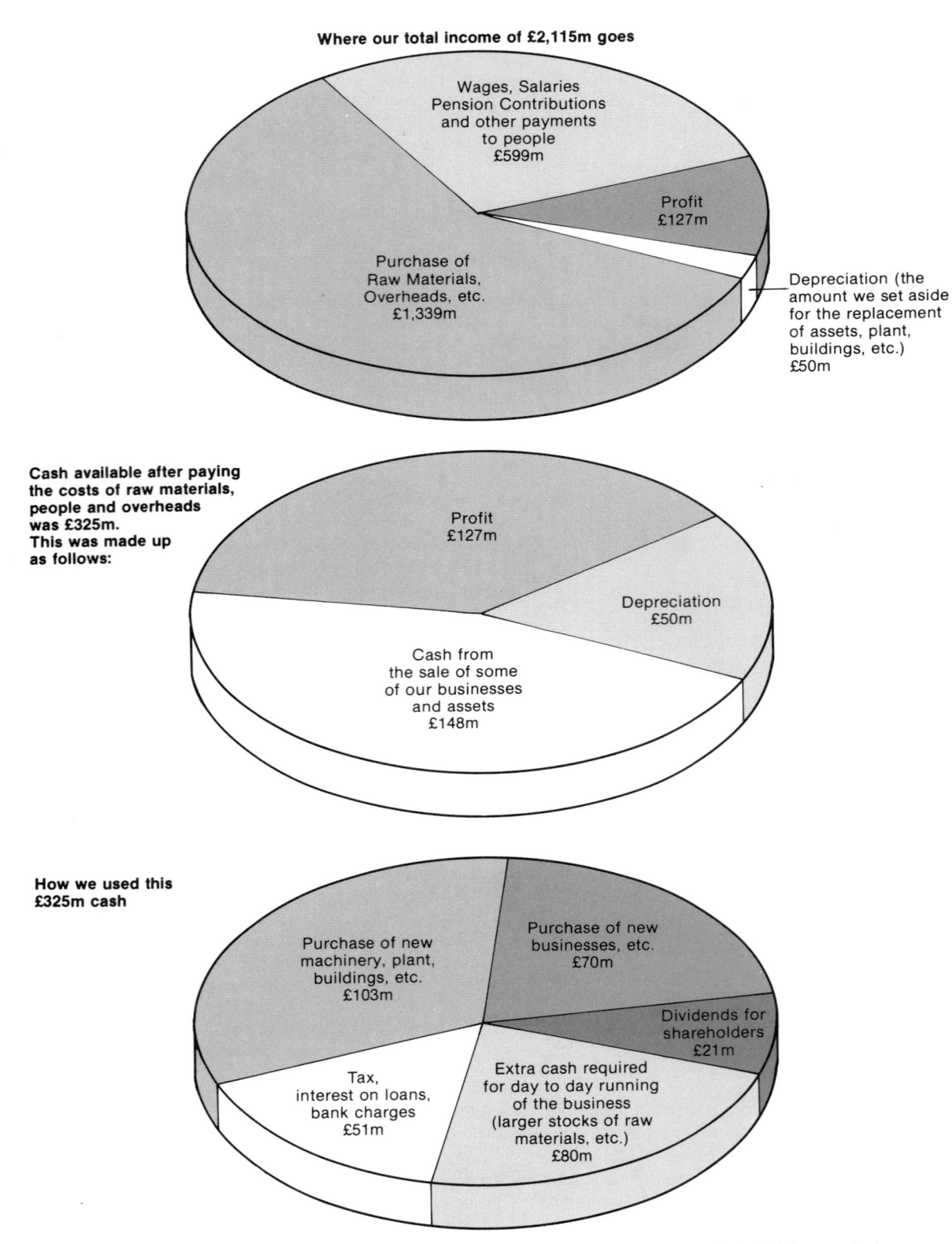

- Wages, Salaries Pension Contributions and other payments to people £599m
- Profit £127m
- Depreciation (the amount we set aside for the replacement of assets, plant, buildings, etc.) £50m
- Purchase of Raw Materials, Overheads, etc. £1,339m

Cash available after paying the costs of raw materials, people and overheads was £325m. This was made up as follows:

- Profit £127m
- Depreciation £50m
- Cash from the sale of some of our businesses and assets £148m

How we used this £325m cash

- Purchase of new machinery, plant, buildings, etc. £103m
- Purchase of new businesses, etc. £70m
- Dividends for shareholders £21m
- Extra cash required for day to day running of the business (larger stocks of raw materials, etc.) £80m
- Tax, interest on loans, bank charges £51m

The figures for the year to 31 March 1985 are abridged from the Group's full accounts for that period, which have received an unqualified auditors' report and will be filed with the Registrar of Companies after the Annual General Meeting.

ducts are *Woman's Own, Amateur Gardening,* Crown paints, Polyfilla and *Country Life.* Reed also runs Butterworth Publishers.

Many thousands of people are employed by Reed International. This means that the staff could be forgiven for thinking they are small cogs in a complex machine.

Each year, Reed produces two reports. One is the Annual Report, a booklet on all the main businesses, illustrated in colour, with full financial details of the year's trading figures. The second is an Employee Report, equally well illustrated, but taking a slightly different theme – the company's position as seen from the viewpoint of the staff rather than investors and customers.

Using pie-charts (see facing page), Reed explains to employees how the 1984–5 sales income of £2115 million was spent.

Look at the charts and answer these questions.

Questions

1 Out of the income of £2115 million, how much went
   (a) in wages and salaries?
   (b) to purchase raw materials and on overheads?
   (c) in depreciation? Explain what this means.
   (d) in profit?
2 How did Reed use the £325 million cash available? How much was
   (a) paid in tax and loans and bank charges?
   (b) used to purchase new machinery and buildings?
   (c) paid as dividends to shareholders?

Government and business

25
Private and public sectors

Private enterprise

'Private enterprise' means the goods and services which are manufactured or provided by private companies, partnerships or individuals. These goods (which are usually sold in shops or direct to the public), and the services (insurance, transport, repairs etc) are offered for sale on the basis that customers can decide whether or not to buy and they can choose from different makes or services. This is the 'private sector' of industry.

The public sector

'Public sector' goods and services are provided by three kinds of organisation which have a right and a monopoly to provide certain services. These are:
Public corporations e.g. electricity boards, the BBC, the Post Office.

Central government services. These are services which come under the control of a government department such as the Department of Health and Social Security which is responsible for:
- hospitals and medical services.
- social services such as pensions, youth training, job centres etc.

Local government services. These are social centres (residential homes for the elderly, childrens' centres, etc); roads; waste disposal; police; libraries and recreation, and education.

Public corporations

These are large organisations set up by parliament to make sure that important services are provided for the public benefit. The corporations are responsible for running their own businesses and offer services such as broadcasting, gas, electricity. They are controlled by parliament and the government. Because they are public services, the corporations are responsible to a minister, and they cannot spend money unless it is agreed by parliament.

Each corporation has a Board of Directors. As long as they run the business efficiently and do not get into debt, the Boards are able to run the day-to-day business.

Nationalised industries

These are industries which at one time were in the hands of private companies. After 1945, they were taken over by the Government, or 'nationalised'. It was felt by the Labour Government of the time that services and industries such as coal, iron and steel, and the railways, should be run for the benefit of everyone, not just shareholders. For some time, however, these industries were run at a loss, for massive amounts of money were needed for investment in order to modernise them. This was another reason for nationalisation – to overhaul and bring up-to-date the major industries of Britain.

In the 1980s, industries such as gas and electricity began to make large profits and this helped to finance new developments. The Conservative Government, which had never supported nationalisation, decided to 'sell off' sections of nationalised industry. In 1984 shares in British Telecom were put on sale allowing private investors to own part of a major industry.

There have been occasions, too, when large and important private industries have had to be taken over by the Government (even Conservative governments) to save them from bankruptcy. This happened with British Leyland, the car manufacturer, and most of the shipbuilding industry. The government is then able to invest money for the recovery of these essential industries.

Nationalisation . . . or not?

There are arguments for and against nationalising industries. Some people say that if we put a major industry into the hands of the State, it takes away the incentive to work hard and make a profit. There is, after all, no competition: only one supplier of gas or electricity, and the Post Office only has rivals for certain express services.

On the other hand, other people say that essential services cannot be left to private individuals, and if big profits are to be made, they should be for everyone's benefit, or so heavily taxed (as in the case of the oil industry) that profits can help to pay for Britain's social services.

Governments have different views on 'privatization' of industry. At present, the Conservative government is considering a number of industries for privatization. These include the water boards, gas boards and the forestry commission.

Questions

1 Make a list of (a) public corporations, and (b) nationalised industries.
2 Write out a list of arguments *for* nationalisation. Then write down several reasons to explain why in the past different governments have supported or taken over various industries completely or have taken a major share in them.

Where are the workers?

About 20 per cent of the possible UK workforce are employed by the government in the civil service or other jobs (including the Armed Forces), in local government (including the police and education), and the national health service. Another 5 per cent are employed in nationalised industries and by public corporations.

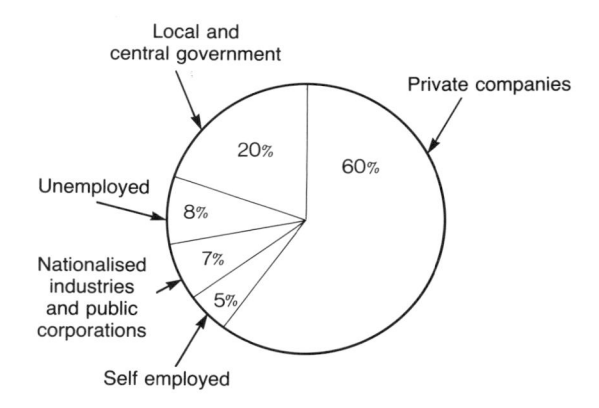

Let's look at the distribution of labour as a whole. The pie-chart shows that the proportion of the workforce employed in private companies is the largest group. However, substantial sectors of the potential workforce *are* employed elsewhere (or not employed at all).

Some services, such as radio and television, are provided partly by public services (the BBC) and partly by private companies (ITV, commercial radio).

Can you think of any reasons why it could be a good idea to offer the same or similar services through private enterprise and by public corporations?

Find out how the following goods and services are provided, or the natural resources are controlled. Is it by a public corporation, private companies, local or central government services?

insurance	dog licenses
newspapers	petrol
the fire services	bicycles
law courts	supplementary benefit
water supply	libraries

Who decides?

Decisions on whether services will be organised locally or centrally, or allowed to pass into the hands of private business are taken by governments. In the last 40 years, some governments have favoured close central control through Parliament. At other times, local government authorities have been given a lot of freedom to arrange things to suit local needs.

In the 1980s, the pendulum swung back to central direction and control. This is done by central government fixing the 'spending limits' for local authorities and the boards of public corporations, and by checking up on them through the departments of state – the Departments of Employment, Environment, Health and Social Services, Education etc. First of all, the Treasury – the most powerful government department, sets spending targets. This means that for the coming financial year, each government department is told the maximum amount that can be spent on housing, health, nationalised industries etc. The 'money' is the total government revenue which comes from taxes and other sources.

In turn, the local authorities and public corporations are told how much they can spend in a year. After that, it is up to the local authority to find most of the money from rates and other income. The government itself chips in. The whole of the spending budget for a nationalised industry may come from its income, for instance in the case of the gas and electricity industries. But local authorities have to be 'topped up' and this is done by means of the Rate Support Grant which the government pays to each local authority to help pay for police, education and its other services.

Let's look at an example of one 'service' – housing. In 1984, the Government, through the Treasury, fixed a total sum to be spent on the construction and improvement of council housing. The sum was £3055 million – a lot of money. But it was *less* than the local authorities expected. Therefore, many local plans had to be changed, with 'cutbacks' in new projects, and this caused a storm of protest both in Parliament and in the country. But, as the Government pointed out, all these plans have to be *paid for*. And the money to pay the bills comes from rates and taxes. So if a county council wants to spend more on housing, it should be prepared to increase rates and to agree to rises in income and other taxes which may not be a popular policy with electors who live in the area.

The decision-makers

Britain is a democratic country. The decision-makers are elected. In London, they are the hundred or so men and women who make up the Government, led by the Prime Minister and the Cabinet. Then there are the major departments of state, each one led by a minister who is a Member of Parliament, and therefore elected. Next, there are over 400 000 officials whose job is to carry out the decisions of government. This is the Civil Service, which plays a leading part in decision-making.

In public corporations, it is the Board of Directors who are responsible for policy. But they can be overthrown or forced to change their policy by Parliament.

In local government, it is the elected councillors who decide important topics. The officials of the council are there to carry out those decisions.

It should be clear, therefore, that decision-taking is a complex business, and before any important decision is taken, there is generally a lot of discussion in committees, in newspapers, and in Parliament. That's how democracy works. It can be very slow, and mistakes can be made. But it gives a chance for the general public, that's you and me, to make our opinions known. If we don't like the decision, there's always the next election, when the decision-makers will again be trying to win our approval and support.

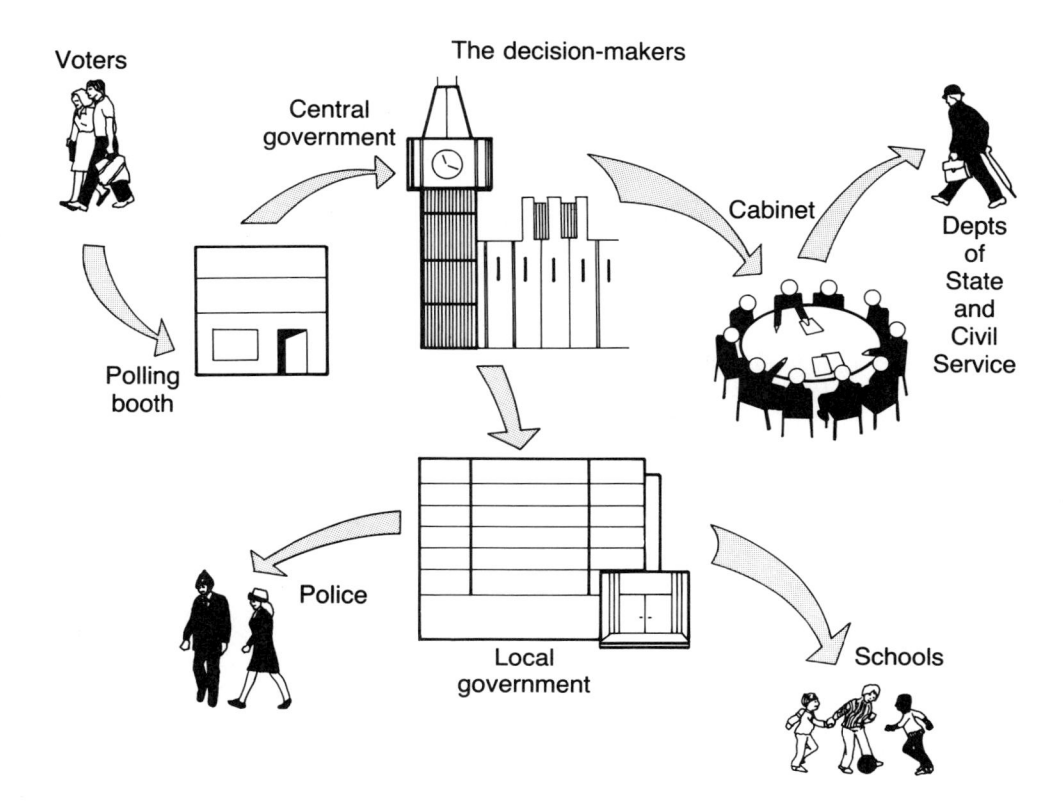

Questions

1 Give an example of a decision which could be made by these decision-makers:
   (a) a voter
   (b) the Prime Minister
   (c) the Minister of Defence
   (d) the House of Commons
   (e) a County Council
2 Make a list of some of the people who are decision-makers in Britain. Start with the Queen. Next, the Prime Minister and the Chancellor of the Exchequer. Add more names to your list.
3 Discuss the advantages and disadvantages of the system of decision-making in the UK.

26
Public spending

Every year, in March, the Chancellor of the Exchequer picks up the red despatch box and sets off for the House of Commons to read the budget speech. The House is packed. Television and radio crews are ready. Newspaper reporters are armed with sharpened pencils! The reason for all this interest is that the decisions which the Chancellor takes on Budget Day will affect everyone. Will income tax go up, or down? Will an extra 2p tax be added to the price of beer, cigarettes or petrol? Will VAT (value added tax) be added to the sale of books as well as records?

The Budget is one of the main instruments by which governments influence the nation's economic health. Let's look at the details because it is important to understand how the nation's spending is controlled.

Where does the money go to?

Huge amounts of money are required each year by the government for:

defence	overseas aid
roads and transport	industrial research
industry and trade	agriculture and fisheries
housing	employment services

The chancellor with the despatch box

law and order
public health
education
grants to local authorities
arts, museums and libraries
childrens' services
social security

The total comes to many billions of pounds. This is *expenditure*, and like any other business, the Chancellor has to balance the books by showing how the huge amounts will be balanced by income from various sources.

Where does the money come from?

The main sources are taxes:
- *Direct taxes*, such as *income tax*, subtracted by an employer from an employee's wages and paid direct to the government.
- *Indirect taxes*, these are paid on imports of goods from overseas and also paid by customers through *value added tax* on many of the goods sold in shops.
- *Company taxes*, such as a profits tax called *corporation tax*.

For you to do

Copy this diagram showing government income and expenditure into your notebook. Add extra arrows to show additional ways of getting and spending money.

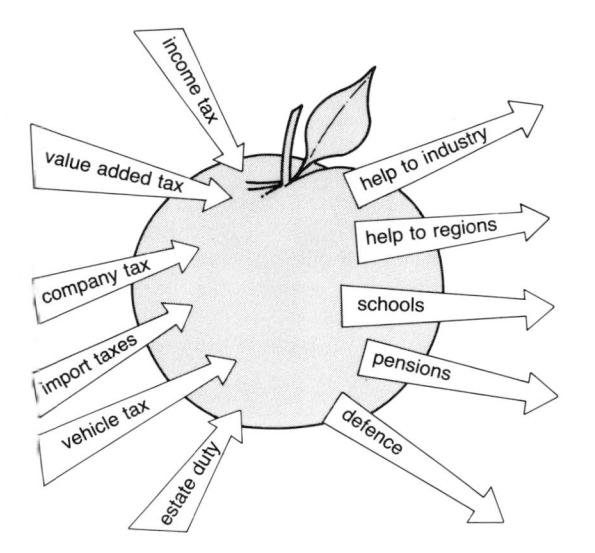

Finance and Parliament

One of Parliament's major tasks is to make arrangements for raising and spending public money. Budget Day is part of this programme. Beforehand, there is a very long process of deciding how much money is needed and where it is coming from.

Although the financial year begins on 1 April, discussions start several months earlier. Over the previous six months, the departments of state prepare their *estimates of spending*. There is a lot of argument. Treasury officials, led by their chief, the Chancellor of the Exchequer, discuss with department ministers and officials how much will be needed for the coming year. The departments usually ask for more than the Treasury will allow. The reason is that each department will have ambitious plans for improving services. But the Treasury takes the nation's view, knowing that the total sum to be spent cannot be any greater than the total income for the government. Otherwise, this would lead to national bankruptcy. Eventually the departments agree terms with the Treasury. The total sums are then published in documents which are presented to Parliament for approval.

Next, the estimates are sent to a committee to be examined in detail. In all, about 30 days are allocated to this work in the Commons. The opposition parties in the Commons usually use this as an opportunity to challenge and criticise the government's spending proposals on, for instance, defence or housing.

The Finance Act

By March, the Chancellor is ready with the budget and the Finance Act. Each year, a new Finance Act has to be passed, making it legal to levy taxes. In the budget speech, the Chancellor considers the financial prospects for the coming year and gives estimates of what is to be spent, and explains whether or not taxes are to be increased. Sometimes it may be possible to reduce taxes, perhaps because of large revenues from the oil industry, but this is unusual.

The proposals that the Chancellor makes in the Budget are put into the Finance Act. This has to be passed by both Houses of Parliament (the House of Commons and the House of Lords) and given the Royal Assent. This can take up to six months, and until the Act becomes law, it is technically illegal to levy taxes.

To help the departments of state (and therefore the government) over this period, Parliament votes on the allocation of money 'on account' – a kind of loan – until the Finance Act becomes law. On Budget night, too, Parliament usually passes 'resolutions' which allow taxes on, say, petrol or beer to take effect immediately, and so the price of petrol at garages can go up on the very next day after the Budget.

Spending in local government

Local authorities, just like central government, have to balance their books. England, Scotland and Wales are divided into over 60 large county councils (Cornwall, Lincolnshire, Strathclyde, Dyfed etc) and there is a similar system for Northern Ireland. Each has a Council which decides on the main lines of policy for the county. These Councils are made up of anything between 40 and over 100 elected members. These are the decision-makers in local government.

The Committee System

Each Council has a set of committees, set up to deal with planning, education, roads, social services, finance and housing. These committees are served by departments of the County Council staffed by permanent full-time officials, led by a Chief Executive and a team of Chief Officers who are the heads of the various departments.

Finance

One of the most important committees in every Council is the Finance Committee. Its job is to balance the books of the County. It can recommend how the money will be spent – so much for libraries, probation service, recreation centres and so on. The Committee is also responsible for recommending how the money will be raised, and this may mean an increase in the rates. The final decisions are taken by the full County Council but it relies heavily on the work done earlier by the Finance Committee.

Hertfordshire County Council

Let's look at a real council to see how this system works. In 1985/86 the Hertfordshire County Council spent £462.5 million (see chart on facing page).

Questions

1 Which service was the biggest spender? What was the annual amount spent on it? Explain why you think that almost *eight times* as much was spent on it than on any other service.
2 What kind of services are provided under highways and waste disposal? (Remember that parts of the M1 and M25 run through Hertfordshire.)
3 Of the £462.5 million total expenditure, how much came from government grants?
4 Apart from rates and grants, what was the other main source of the County's income?

Managing

These vast sums of money require careful management, just as in private business. Perhaps *more* careful managing, because there are councillors and ratepayers looking over the shoulder of the Council's staff. Often there are arguments in the Council and the Finance Committee about priorities. One group of people may say that more should be spent on old people's homes, while another group want to improve roads. A third group of councillors may argue for assistance to industry, in order to provide more employment. Sometimes final decisions are reached only after fierce arguments and votes in the full Council.

Within the County, the main department which deals with finance is the Treasurer's Department. Its job is to provide the Council with financial information and advice and to prepare the annual estimates and accounts. In addition, the Treasurer's Department pays the staff of the Council, meets all bills from suppliers, and collects the income from rates, the government, and other sources.

As you can see, in a democratic society, there are many decision-makers. Members of Parliament, County Councillors, civil servants, local government officers – they all share in the decision-making process. And the business they transact is very big business indeed, for it is the business of a nation.

Manpower

Whole-time Equivalent staff
Education	18,040
Social Services	3,190
Police	2,125
Other Services	3,245
Total Staff	**26,600**

The total number of staff is 50 less than that budgeted for last year; 3,800 less than ten years ago.

Service Staff (teachers etc)	65.4%
Support staff (technicians etc)	28.8%
Administrative staff	5.8%

County population (June 1983)	975,400
Area of County (hectares)	163,400

Expenditure and Income

	£m	£m
Total Expenditure		462.5
Funded from Income:		
Fees & Charges for Services	63.1	
Other Income	26.9	
Government Grants for Specific Services	38.4	
		128.4
Budgeted Expenditure		334.1
less Government Block Grant	60.0	
less Contribution from Balances	5.0	
Leaving:		
to be found from Hertfordshire Ratepayers		269.1
County Rate		157.7p
Rateable Value (April 1984)		£176.4m
Penny Rate Product		£1.72m

Income from ..

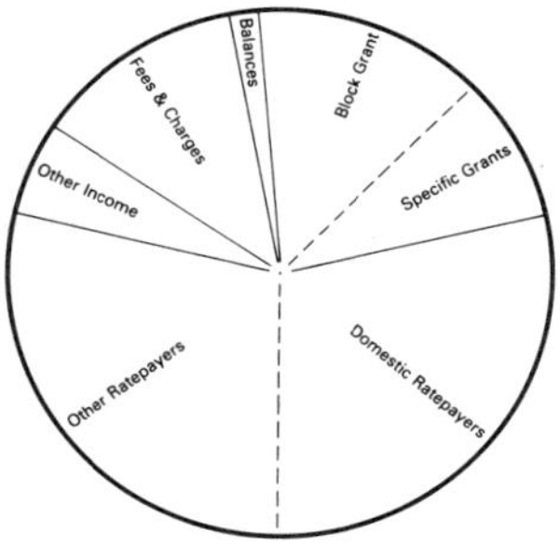

(Pie chart: Fees & Charges, Balances, Block Grant, Specific Grants, Domestic Ratepayers, Other Ratepayers, Other Income)

Service Expenditure

	Gross Expenditure
Education	**£287.4m**
Primary and Nursery Schools. 77,144 pupils 3,488 teachers, 474 schools. Cost per primary pupil £770 net	(£61.2m)
Secondary and Middle Schools. 75,427 pupils 4,896 teachers, 102 schools. Cost per pupil £1,079 net	(£92.3m)
Further Education 1 Polytechnic 9 Colleges of Further Education 4 Specialist Colleges	(£59.2m)

Service Expenditure

	Gross Expenditure
Education contd	
Student Awards 9,749 award holders average value £1,740	(£17.5m)
Other Education Services Special education, youth service, career guidance, milk and meals, administration	(£40.8m)
Contribution to National Advanced Further Education pool	(£16.4m)

..will be spent on ..

(Pie chart: Running expenses (35.0%), Teaching staff (29.8%), Other staff (30.4%), Financing charges (4.8%))

Police	**£37.2m**
1,592 police officers 89 traffic wardens 21 stations, 377 vehicles	
Fire and Public Protection	**£11.3m**
551 whole-time firemen 205* part-time firemen 32 stations 25 trading standards and consumer affairs officers	
Social Services	**£39.9m**
41 day centres 98 residential homes 411 social workers 612* home helps 9 family centres 6 adult training centres	

*Full-time equivalent

	Gross Expenditure
Libraries and Recreation	**£7.0m**
49 libraries, plus archives, recreation and leisure	
Highways & Waste Disposal	**£41.2m**
Motorways and trunk roads: 102 km of motorways, 129 km of trunk roads	(£7.3m)
County Roads 363 km of principal roads, 3,703 km of non principal roads	(£29.1m)
Road Safety	(£0.3m)
Other	(£0.9m)
Waste disposal 325,000 tonnes of waste 18 Household Waste Sites	(£3.6m)

..to provide ..

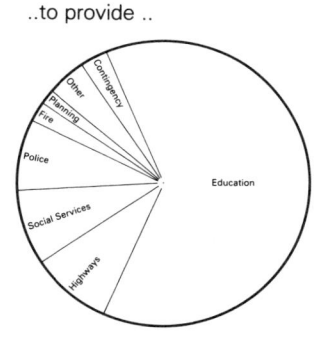

(Pie chart: Contingency, Other, Planning, Fire, Police, Social Services, Highways, Education)

Planning	**£8.2m**
Strategic and local planning	(£2.2m)
Public transport support and co-ordination	(£6.0m)
Other Services	**£14.2m**
Probation, Magistrates Courts, Smallholdings, etc.	

Other Expenditure	**£2.0m**
Land drainage precepts, etc	
Contingency	**£14.1m**
To meet future pay and price increases	
Total Expenditure	**£462.5m**

99

27
Energy, pollution and conservation

Throughout the world there is deep concern about the effects of industrial expansion on people and on the environment. Some of the dramatic and terrifying events of the 1980s have been:
- the escape of poison gas from a fertiliser plant in India, killing and maiming over a thousand people.
- the daily death toll in every industrial country from road traffic accidents.
- disease and death for millions of Africans due to famine.
- sickness and death caused by the escape of radioactive substances into the air, seas and rivers.

These are only four examples. We regularly hear new stories of gas explosions, poison leakages, radiation sickness, industrial cancers, famines and accidents. What we have to ask ourselves is whether this is the result of living in a world where the natural resources are not sufficient to feed everyone, and where the need to obtain and use energy results in damage to health and the environment.

Among the big questions for world leaders (and ourselves) to answer are these:
- How can the poor nations be helped so that famine can be avoided?
- What will happen when the world's energy resources run out?
- How can modern technology be harnessed so that it is not harmful to people?
- How can the world lessen the danger of nuclear warfare?

These questions have to be dealt with if we are to survive on earth. In this chapter we shall look briefly at the causes of some of the problems, and ask you to think about what might be done to cope with the dangers to humanity.

Energy

We shall start with *energy* sources for this is one of the main factors in causing pollution and in creating international tension.

Machines need energy to make them work. In years gone by, the energy first came from *humans* themselves, then *animals* such as the ox and horse, and then from machines.

The first machines harnessed *wind* and *water*. The cotton mills and iron foundaries of 200 years ago used water-wheels to give power to machines. Windmills were used to grind corn. Then, after 1750, *steam* was used to drive machines, and this led to the demand for *coal*. Coal mining thus became a very important industry. As Britain became more and more industrialised, the demand for coal increased. This continued until the end of the 19th century when *electricity* became the driving power for many machines. But the demand for coal continued because coal is needed to drive the generators that create electricity.

Oil is another fossil fuel (like coal). Coal is derived from plants which have been compressed over millions of years. Oil also comes from fossils: tiny sea creatures which were compressed to form pools of oil trapped within rocks. By drilling through the rocks, the oil is released and captured into storage tanks.

Natural gas is often found with oil and this too can be drawn from the earth.

Energy supply

Until 1974, oil was a cheap form of energy. It was produced in the Middle East, USA and South America and shipped to Europe where it was used for burning by industry and in power stations. Then the oil-producing nations suddenly increased their oil prices, creating severe financial problems in western nations. Britain put a lot more effort into prospecting for oil in the North Sea where important deposits were found and exploited.

Nuclear fuels are not fossil fuels. By a complex chemical process, an element called uranium can be processed so that it creates vast amounts of heat. This energy can be exploded (as in atomic bombs) or controlled in order to create energy (as in nuclear power stations).

Wind is used to drive generators which produce electricity. And *water* produces electricity in *hydro-electric stations*. At the moment, these power sources produce only a small proportion of Britain's energy supply, but they could be expanded in the future.

At the present time, experiments are going on to harness more effectively the atmosphere's natural sources of energy – wind, water and sun. However, sunlight cannot be stored and wind and water are unreliable. But as the world moves towards the 21st century, it may be that the sun and space will provide the answers to the search for alternative and safe forms of energy. If not, the industrial world is in for a shock for coal (and therefore electricity) and oil are decreasing resources which will eventually be all used up. And what happens then?

Alternative forms of energy

If and when the traditional forms of fuel run out (estimated to be in about the year 2050) the world will need to have alternative forms of energy.

One possibility is wider use of *nuclear power*. However, at the present time nuclear energy is not proving to be as useful as was expected. It is a very complex and expensive process to create electricity within a nuclear reactor. About 10 per cent of Britain's energy comes from this source. In the future, therefore, scientific breakthroughs will be needed in order to make this a cheaper and more efficient form of energy. Secondly, the creation of nuclear power has its dangers and there are many people who think it should be stopped.

The sun's rays (*solar power*) can be used to heat water into steam. You may have heard about experiments with mirrors and lenses to harness the sun. However, there are problems. There's not too much sun at night, and Britain does have its fair share of cloudy days! The biggest problem, however, is the weakness of the power. For instance, it takes a glass mirror one metre square 12 hours to produce enough power to light a single light bulb.

Assignment

Here is a diagram to show the solar-heated house of the 21st century. Make a list of the ways that heat is created and is conserved in this house. Re-draw your own house to show how heat could be obtained and used from the sun and the wind, and how heat might be better sealed into the house rather than be allowed to escape.

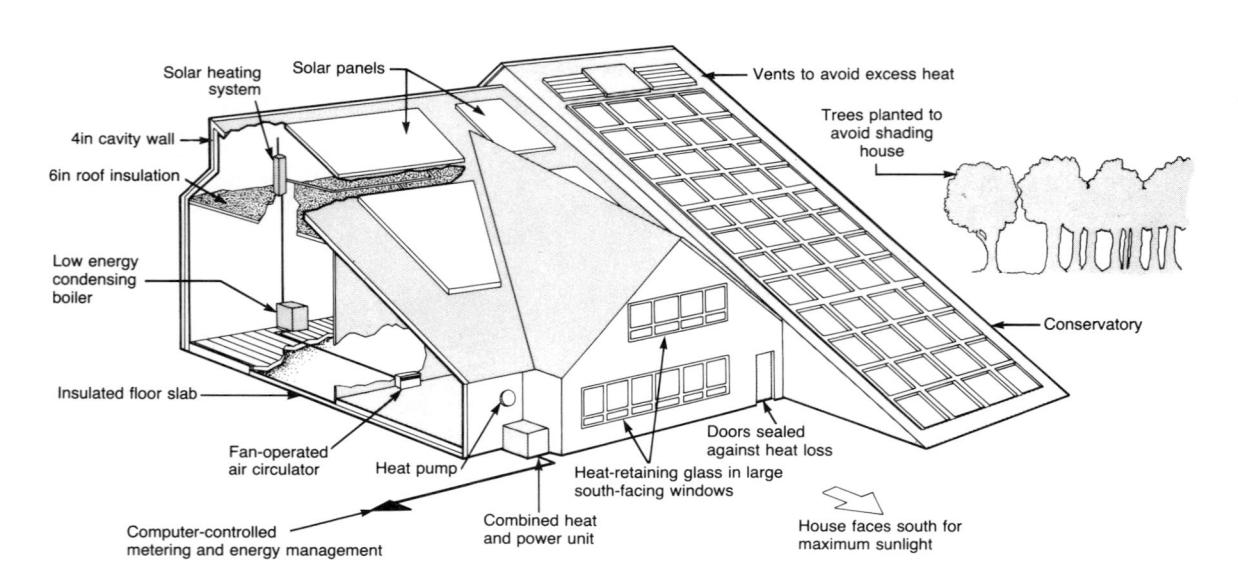

Questions

In your notebook draw this chart. On the left hand side, make a list of the main forms of energy. In two other columns, list the advantages and disadvantages of each.

Energy	Advantages	Disadvantages
coal	sufficient supply in Britain to last to the year 2050	expensive to mine

Pollution

Pollution isn't new. Many of the buildings of Britain's towns and cities have recently been cleaned to get rid of the black stain caused by coal-burning fires. The Clean Air Act of 1956 made it illegal to burn coal in smokeless zones in cities, and this has greatly helped to improve the quality of life there.

However, rivers, lakes, the sea and the air are still affected by pollution. To take only one example when you see smoke rising from car exhausts, power stations and oil refineries, it allows sulphur dioxide and other chemicals to seep into the atmosphere. When the chemicals react with the air, they release 'acid rain' which has been known to kill fish in lakes, shorten the life of trees, and damage stone buildings. In West Germany, for example, a third of the forests have been affected by acid rain.

Radioactive pollution is another great danger. Leukaemia and cancer can be caused by it. The pollution began when tests were conducted on

Hiroshima after the bomb. Nuclear power grows despite horrific memories

atomic explosions, culminating in the atomic bombs dropped on the Japanese cities of Hiroshima and Nagasaki in 1945. Since then, because of weapons tests, the higher levels of the atmosphere have become polluted with radioactivity.

On the ground, another dangerous source of pollution is from the waste of nuclear power stations such as Sellafield in Cumbria. The plant pumps radioactive waste into the Irish Sea through a pipeline, and there have been serious accidents along the coast and concern over the pollution of the beaches etc.

Pollution from farming

Some of the chemicals used to improve crops have also caused pollution. Among the chemicals are *pesticides* (to kill insects) and *herbicides* (to kill weeds). *Fertilizers* (used to help plants to grow) have dangerous effects, too. The manufacture of these substances has caused tragedies such as the escape of poison gas from a fertilizer plant in Bhopal in India in 1984. In Britain, about 1 400 000 tons of nitrate fertilizer are spread on the fields each year. These chemicals can have a dangerous effect on human beings if they get into the water supply.

Asbestos

Thirty years ago, people thought it was quite safe to use asbestos to insulate all kinds of buildings, including schools, hospitals, offices and factories. It has only recently been discovered that asbestos is very dangerous and can cause cancer. As a result, asbestos linings are being taken from all buildings, but it will take years before the work is finally finished.

Lead

Lead is added to petrol to improve the performance of car engines. But lead is a dangerous poison and when it gets into the air from vehicle exhaust fumes it can cause disease. The government has asked oil companies to stop putting lead into petrol and in the USA there are laws which make all car manufacturers ensure that engines are run on lead-free petrol.

Water pollution

It has been calculated that each person in Britain uses over 30 gallons of water each day for drinking, cooking, washing, cleaning clothes and flushing the lavatory. To this should be added the 30 gallons a day used by industry for every person in the UK. Water is, of course, in constant circulation. It falls as rain, is collected in reservoirs, is used for drinking or washing, is returned to rivers and the sea, and evaporates into the air to create more rain.

Water is essential to animal and human life. If it is polluted by the release of chemicals into it, fish and other water creatures will suffer and die. Industrial waste products poison water, and this is the reason for the very careful control over sewage deposited in the sea and rivers. Human sewage, like industrial waste products, has to be treated so that it does not damage the environment for us and animals.

Land pollution

There are still remnants of the industrial revolution in Britain's countryside – slag heaps, waste tips, quarries. But these are gradually being demolished or filled in. In the 20th century, there is a new form of land pollution – corporation rubbish tips. Such is the volume of refuse from houses, offices and industry that local authorities have to spend huge sums of money on collecting rubbish. It is possible, by spending further amounts of money, to turn this waste into sludge which can be spread on the land to improve it. However, as a stop-gap, local councils dump industrial and domestic waste into holes or on tips, and in recent years there have been several cases of chemical poisons and explosions on waste areas, caused by dangerous substances reacting with each other.

The law moves in

What should be done? To avoid pollution, a new law was passed in 1974, the Control of Pollution Act. This made it illegal to dump waste in rivers, lakes and the sea, or to put it into holes in the ground, unless permission had been given by the Water Board or the Environmental Health Department of the local authority. People who have ignored this law have been prosecuted.

Local authorities are responsible for getting rid of waste. The government, too, is responsible, through the Department of the Environment. But a particular problem has arisen in recent years over nuclear waste. At present, nuclear waste is held in barrels and there are problems of what to do with it, because a speck of plutonium can kill, even after hundreds of years underground. A serious international incident occurred in 1984 when a French ship sank in the North Sea, releasing barrels of nuclear waste into the sea. If that happened again and the waste escaped, it could cause a terrible disaster.

What examples of pollution are there in this drawing? What other examples of pollution could be added to the picture?

A great deal has been achieved by ordinary people, especially when they have joined organisations such as Greenpeace and Friends of the Earth. These groups are fighting to protect the environment from industrial damage. Ordinary people can help in many ways. One is to avoid polluting the air or the land by dropping litter waste or by unnecessary car journeys. And if you see examples of pollution, complain to the authority in charge.

Questions and assignments

1 Make a list of the ways by which you think that companies, local authorities and the government might seek to avoid polluting the air, the land and the sea.
2 Discuss in your group what the main forms of energy are likely to be in the 21st century.
3 List the major causes of air pollution and say what has been done to control the release of harmful substances into the atmosphere.
4 In what ways can pesticides, herbicides and fertilizers cause pollution?
5 What are the dangers from nuclear waste, and what should be done to control the use of nuclear power?

Conservation

The information provided in this chapter, added to your own reading, should have indicated that the world is in great danger. One way of combatting the drain on natural resources is to avoid waste, and to *conserve* or protect these resources.

To make power and energy sources last longer, we must use less coal, oil, electricity and gas. This is why the government is constantly encouraging people to 'save energy' although it is in *everyone's* interests to do so, because it also saves money from the household budget.

To avoid wastage of heat, we are encouraged to insulate houses, offices, shops and factories. For an initial outlay on double-glazing or (as in the case of factories) computer-controlled energy use, it is possible to make substantial long-term savings.

It is not only oil, coal and gas which will run out. Eventually the raw supply of materials which are used in industry will be used up. It is expected that the world supply of zinc will run out by 1990, tin and copper by 2000, and aluminium and iron within another 40 years after that. Manufacturing companies and scientists are therefore trying hard to find alternative materials. Among them are plastics, fibre-glass and chemically produced clothing fibres. But this isn't the answer, either, because oil is used to make plastics and coal is needed for the manufacture of many products.

Recycling useful resources

Apart from conserving essential raw materials, and cutting down on waste, another method of conservation is by *recycling* which means re-using materials a second (and more) times, instead of throwing them away.

You may see a special container in a parking area or near shops called a 'Bottle Bank'. People are encouraged to put their used bottles into the container. In this way the glass is saved to be used again. This is an example of recycling.

Some articles such as newspapers, plastic cutlery, paper plates and disposable nappies are designed to be used once and thrown away. This is very wasteful. Newspapers can be used again, and some charities collect them and sell the paper. It's difficult to imagine a new use for a nappy, but the day may come! Newspapers, bottles, cardboard and the hundreds of different kinds of packaging for goods bought in shops and stores are all disposable products, and it is wasteful to destroy them.

To cope with this problem, the public ought perhaps to avoid buying disposable goods and to reject something sold in a huge cardboard box. But as we have seen in earlier parts of this book, companies use packaging as a means of attracting customers to buy their goods.

Recycling has become more sophisticated. For instance, when a car is a wreck, the iron can be melted down and used again. Waste food from restaurants is taken away, sometimes to feed pigs, sometimes to be recycled into fertilizers.

Questions

1 In your notebook, explain in your own words what these words mean: *conservation, insulation, recycling*.
2 Make a list of the things that you now throw away that could be recycled. When selecting items for use later, the sorters select different parts – wood, iron, other metals, paper and cardboard, glass, foodstuffs. Do this for the waste items you have thought of.
3 Pick out three examples of packaging. Consider their use. Was this packaging needed for safety, protection or hygiene? How could they have been less wastefully packaged?

28
Personal incomes . . . and how they are spent

Your 'personal income' is how much you are paid for your work. If an employer says, 'I'll pay you £80 a week to do this job', in theory that's what you *earn*. In theory *only*. In fact, you'll *actually* receive a good deal less than £80. Then, when you have the money in your hand, you can begin to spend it.

Very often, most of it will have to go on three necessities – warmth, shelter and food. After that, there's clothes, transport and household goods. If you have anything left by the time you have paid for these items, you can begin to think of luxury goods such as TV, radio, records, a car etc.

Who decides your income?

You may be fortunate and decide your own income. But that's only true of self-employed people. Over 90 per cent of the working population (and 100 per cent of non-working people) depend on someone else to make that decision. Some workers are on a *flat-rate* wage: that is, they are paid at a standard rate for the job – £5 an hour, let's say. Others may be on *piece-work* which means that a price or rate is fixed for each job, related to how many hours have been given in which to complete it. Then there's *overtime* rates, perhaps at 'time and a half' which means that if you are paid £4 an hour as a normal rate, overtime will be paid at £6 an hour.

An alternative way of arranging payment is by *salary*. Under this system, an employee's pay is decided on an annual figure, say £8500 a year. The usual method of payment is monthly, so the employee would be entitled to twelve monthly payments of £708.34.

Taxation

We have seen that taxes are essential to create the revenue to pay for essential services. On the other hand, no one enjoys paying tax. So, in order to lessen the pain of paying, deductions are made 'at source' which means that (in the case of income tax) it is deducted by the employer and passed direct to the tax authorities.

Income tax

Everyone who earns money above the *minimum allowance* pays income tax. The allowance is the amount of money which a person is allowed to earn before paying tax. In 1985–6, for example, the allowance was £2205 for a single person and £3458 for a married person. The allowance is usually increased each year. The basic rate of tax is at present 30 per cent, but this is also liable to change, depending on the government's decision.

To work out how much tax you would pay, you have to take your allowance off the total pay (this is the *gross* pay) and multiply the remainder by 30p.

For example, if you are paid, say, £100 a week this comes to £5200 a year. The single person's allowance is £2205. So the sum looks like this:

```
    £
  5200
- 2205
  ----
  2995    £2995 × 30p = £898.50
```

You would pay £898.50 a year in tax, which is £17.28 a week.

Our £100 a week earner has therefore already paid over £17 in tax and there's more to come!

National Insurance

There's another direct tax still to be paid. (A direct tax is deducted from what you earn, before you are paid.) This is National Insurance. The weekly payments are taken off a person's wages by the employer who adds on the employer's contribution, and passes the total amount to a government department. These payments go towards the cost of National Insurance benefits – sickness benefit, old age pensions, unemployment benefit, and so on.

NI contributions are calculated according to how much a person earns. People earning £100 a week pay around £8. High earners with £300 a week would pay about £18 a week.

Indirect taxes

These taxes are paid on things we buy. The main ones are VAT and excise duties.

Value Added Tax (VAT) is a tax paid on the shop price of many goods and services. Some items are exempt, such as food, although 'take-away foods' are now VAT-rated. The rate is 15 per cent, which means that the tax is added to the price you pay.

To take an example, if a plumber is called in to your house to repair broken pipes, you are likely to be presented with a bill like this:

cost of materials	£24
labour	£ 8
Sub total	£32
plus VAT at 15%	£ 4.80
Grand total	£36.80

In shops, you aren't likely to see VAT added to the bill. But the store will already have absorbed the 15% in the price, so you won't escape paying it. VAT is paid direct by the shop or supplier to HM Customs and Excise.

Excise duties

These are additional taxes paid on some items, such as cigarettes, perfume, tobacco, petrol, beer and spirits. When you go abroad, you can buy some of these goods at the Duty Free shops at airports and seaports without the extra excise duty payment. You will notice the difference in price.

Special taxes and licences

The government also sets special taxes such as the Road Fund tax which is paid by a car owner. At present it is £100 for a year, but like all other taxes, this can be altered by Parliament. Licences are another form of taxation, such as television licences and dog licences.

Local taxes

The queue of people able to deduct money from your income is already a long one. The earner with £100 a week has now paid income tax and NI contributions. If he or she is a member of a contributory pension scheme, another payment (perhaps 5 or 6 per cent of salary) will be deducted before the weekly wage packet or monthly salary cheque is handed over.

Then, if the family has a car, TV and a dog, they are liable for other taxes.

Before long, however, another tax demand may come through the letterbox. This may be in the form of a *rate demand*. As you have seen, local authorities pay for schools, roads, water, sewage, parks, local transport etc. About half of the money needed to run these services comes from the rates. Every house has a *rateable value* which is estimated on how much rent could be charged if the house was to be let to someone. The bigger the house, the higher the rateable value. Each year, having worked out how much money is needed, the local authority fixes a *rate* which is the proportion of the rateable value each householder will have to pay for the year. For example:

rateable value of the house	£600
rate for the year	£1.34
rates to be paid	£600 × 1.34 = £804

There are arguments *for* and *against* rates as a form of local taxation. One of the objections is that rates do not take into account how many earners live in the house. For example, if a single person lives alone, then the whole burden falls on one person. The house next door may have four wage-earners: father, mother and two grown-up children.

Company taxes

As we have seen in previous chapters, companies also pay taxes. Apart from corporation and other forms of taxation, all employers pay a National Insurance contribution for each employee. They also pay rates to the local authority.

Questions

1 In your own words, explain what is meant by direct and indirect taxes, and give three examples of each.
2 Instead of the rates system, suggest other ways by which local taxes could be raised, or explain other ways of paying for local services.

Benefits

There are two kinds of benefits and allowances available.
- Those to which everyone is entitled no matter what their income, such as old age pensions, family allowances and sickness benefit. These are called *universal* benefits.
- Those that depend on income. Among these are free school meals, family income supplement, supplementary benefit. These are

called *means-tested* benefits.

There are over 40 means-tested grants. Family income supplement, for example, is paid to families where the family income falls below a minimum level set by the government. Free dental and optical treatment is available for people whose income is low.

The system of benefits and allowances can in times of inflation combine to force low-paid people into what has become known as the 'poverty trap'. This happens when a pay increase for the wage-earner in the family is cancelled out by lost entitlement to benefits as the income cut-off point has been reached. For example:

Tom Bell earns £80 a week. He is married with two children. If he gets a pay rise of 10 per cent (£8), he could lose the following benefits:
- free school meals
- family income supplement
- free health treatment
- rent rebate

The reason? His pay rise has taken his wage beyond the level of state support. Don't forget, too, that Tom will be paying income tax on his pay rise, plus extra national insurance contributions, so he could be *worse off*.

What do you think?

Discuss these questions in groups.

1 Suppose it has been decided by the government that this year everyone will be given the same flat-rate pay rise of 6%.
   This means that someone earning £80 a week gets an increase of £4.80, and someone on £400 a week gets £24. Is this fair or unfair?
2 Many state benefits are 'transfer payments' which means that, in effect, the well-off (through high taxation) contribute far more to unemployment benefit. Is this fair or unfair?
3 How could the 'poverty trap' be avoided?
4 What is the best way of taxing people – by direct taxes or by indirect taxes?

How we spend our money . . . .

This chart, which shows household spending in 1984, contains some interesting facts. Study the chart and answer these questions.

1 If the household's income is £60 a week, what percentage goes on the three necessities of housing, food and heating? What is the percentage for the highest income group on £300 a week?

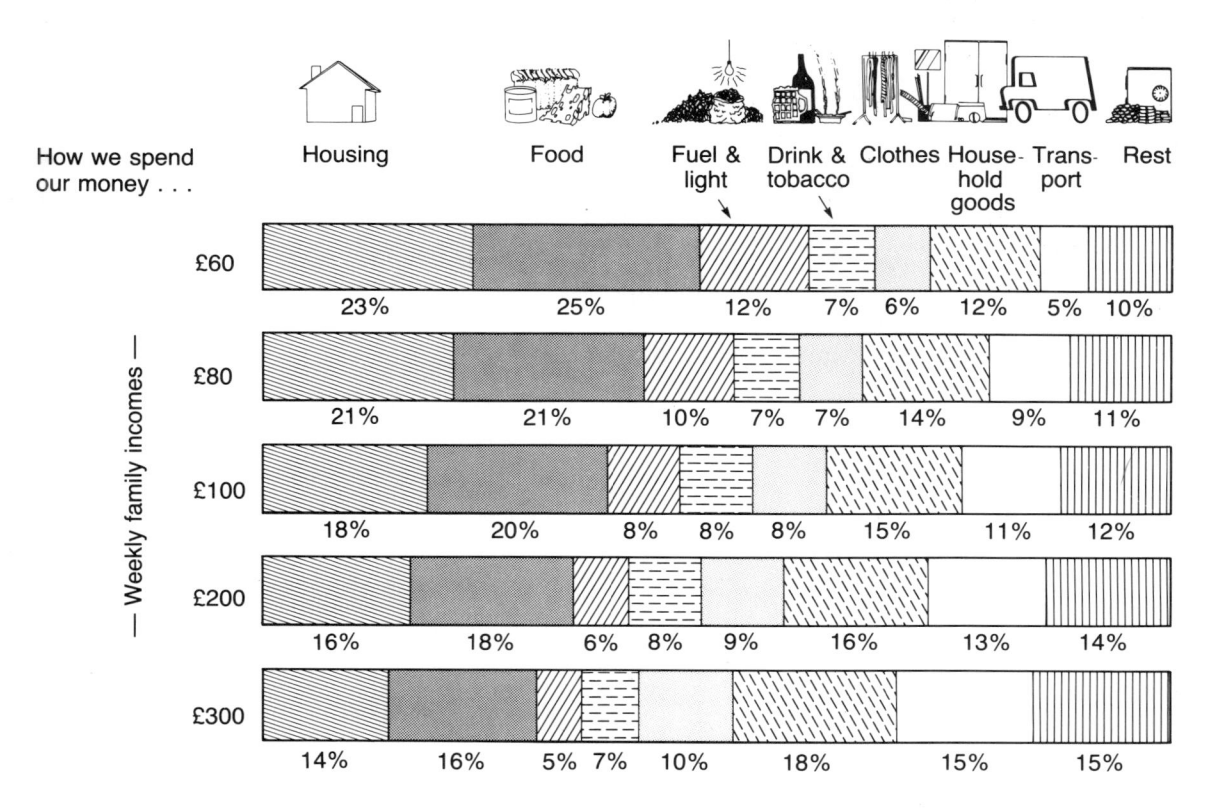

How we spend our money . . .

— Weekly family incomes —

Income	Housing	Food	Fuel & light	Drink & tobacco	Clothes	Household goods	Transport	Rest
£60	23%	25%	12%	7%	6%	12%	5%	10%
£80	21%	21%	10%	7%	7%	14%	9%	11%
£100	18%	20%	8%	8%	8%	15%	11%	12%
£200	16%	18%	6%	8%	9%	16%	13%	14%
£300	14%	16%	5%	7%	10%	18%	15%	15%

2 What do you notice about transport costs and drink and tobacco costs?

3 What other conclusions do *you* come to in looking at this chart?

The main conclusion must be that the poorer you are, the greater the percentage of your income has to go on necessities. People in the lowest bracket have to spend 60% keeping warm, fed and housed. The higher earners also spend more than three times as much on transport.

In 1983, household spending in Britain went up by 6.5%. However, this means that the gap is widening between rich and poor, employed and unemployed. For most of this increase in spending was within the higher income groups.

The distribution of personal wealth

Wealthy people do not keep very much of their wealth in the form of money. The Inland Revenue has estimated that people with wealth between £500 000 and a million pounds hold less than £5 in every £1000 as money, which means cash at home or in a current account at the bank.

What do they do with it?

Let's take £500 000. Of this, £5000 is likely to be in the form of money at the bank or at home; £150 000 is in property; £45 000 is in deposit accounts, pension schemes and building societies, and the remaining £300 000 in stocks and shares or personal business commitments.

Let's look at it another way. The top 10% of salary-earners in this country take home 30% of the national wage bill. This same 10% also happen to own 75% of the wealth (land, housing, shares, companies) of the UK. The bottom 50% (half the population) earn 25% of the total pay of the nation and own about 1% of the total wealth.

Discuss

1 Do you think it is fair that the wealth of Britain (or any other country in the West) is concentrated in a few hands?

2 Read these case-studies. Do you agree or disagree with the questions about them? Discuss your opinions within the group.

(a) Mr and Mrs Smith worked hard all their lives. They paid off the mortgage on their home, they saved carefully, and when they died, left everything to their two grown-up children, Alice and Rob. All together, taking the value of the house, Alice and Rob inherited £80 000 which they divided equally.

   (i) Is it right that the two children should get this money if they did not earn it?

(b) When Lord Southdown died, he left an estate valued at £1 600 000. This included the value of his country house which has been owned by the family for 200 years. Death duties tax took £500 000. In order to pay this tax, and avoid having to sell the family home, Lord Southdown's two children, Lord Jim and Lady Jane sold off the family's art collection for £600 000. The whole of the collection went to the USA.

   (i) Is it right that Lord Jim and Lady Jane should inherit this fortune? What is the difference, if any, between the Southdown inheritance and the Smith family inheritance?

   (ii) Is it right that death duties should be paid on the Southdown estate?

   (iii) Is it right that in order to pay the government tax, valuable art paintings which had been in Britain for many years should go to the USA?

29
Money and inflation or how the government seeks to control the economy

For the last 40 years, all governments, whether Conservative or Labour, have had these economic objectives.
- *Full employment*, which means plenty of jobs and low unemployment.
- *A low rate of inflation*, with strict controls over price increases.
- *Economic expansion*, with the growth of new industries to replace older ones.
- *Increasing foreign trade*, with Britain exporting goods of more value than it imports.

But, in fact, in these 40 years Britain has suffered from the *exact opposite* of these objectives.
- *High unemployment*. (In 1986 it reached 3.4 million.)
- *A high rate of inflation*. For example, in 1974 prices rose by 19% and wages by 29%.
- *Economic decline*, with falling output from industry, especially in steel, coal and the railways.
- *A deficit balance of payments*, in which Britain imported more goods than were exported. (In 1974 the deficit was £15 000 million.)

How did this happen? What went wrong? To discover the answers, let us look at some recent government economic policies in a little more detail.

Inflation

This is simply the result of paying ourselves too much. In the 1970s some powerful trade unions negotiated wage increases much higher than the cost of living. Companies had to recover their costs by raising the prices of their goods. With higher prices for British goods, overseas customers were reluctant to buy, so overseas trade declined. Governments added to inflation by increasing taxes, such as petrol duty and VAT, which directly increased prices. Another twist to inflation at this time came when overseas investors, losing confidence in Britain, sold British currency, so reducing the value of the pound compared with the US dollar and other currencies.

In the 1980s, the main government objective has been to control inflation. This was done and the rate of inflation fell from 20% in 1978 to 5% in 1985. But to achieve this, other policies had to be put on the shelf.

Imports

Britain depends very heavily on imported raw materials (see diagram over page). But, between 1970 and 1975, the price of imports rose by over 100 per cent and oil prices quadrupled. The consequence was that more and more money was paid to Japan, the USA, West Germany and other overseas countries. In the same period, British exports could not expand at anything like the same level, so the *balance of payments* gradually became worse.

The balance of payments means the costs of imports are set against those of exports. Put another way, for every two pounds that we spend on British goods and services, we spend one pound on imported goods from abroad. Should we be putting all this money into the hands of foreigners? German cars, Japanese cameras, shirts from Portugal, shoes from Italy, – why don't we make our own goods?

The answer is that we can obtain these goods *more cheaply* from overseas. The answer to the balance of payments (given by economists) is that there is little point in trying to produce and sell the same goods that can be made more cheaply in Hong Kong and elsewhere. What we should be doing is to *specialise* in products such as electronics, robotics, chemicals and other areas of technology which call for a high degree of technical skill.

The money supply

The Bank of England and some Scottish banks are the only manufacturers of money. But the government controls the amount and the supply of money by issuing orders to all banks.

In the last 40 years, some governments have been spending more money than they collected

What we import

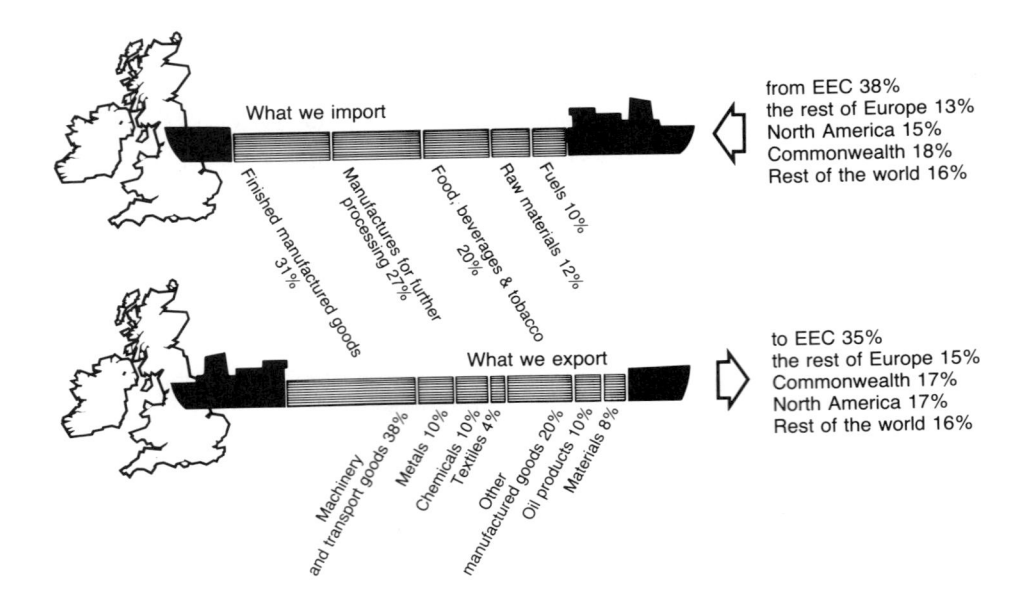

Finished manufactured goods 31%
Manufactures for further processing 27%
Food, beverages & tobacco 20%
Raw materials 12%
Fuels 10%

from EEC 38%
the rest of Europe 13%
North America 15%
Commonwealth 18%
Rest of the world 16%

What we export

Machinery and transport goods 38%
Metals 10%
Chemicals 10%
Textiles 4%
Other manufactured goods 20%
Oil products 10%
Materials 8%

to EEC 35%
the rest of Europe 15%
Commonwealth 17%
North America 17%
Rest of the world 16%

in taxes. The gap was met by printing more paper money, and by borrowing from the banks. Easy, but dangerous. For the effect of this policy is to increase the already huge debt and to put more money into circulation, which again fans inflation.

In the early 1980s, the Government put strict controls on the money supply and on government spending. But this had other consequences including cuts in government spending on roads, the health service, education and so on. Another consequence was higher unemployment.

Unemployment and inflation

Which is worse – inflation or unemployment? We worry about inflation because it:
* eats away our savings.
* leads to rising prices.
* makes it more difficult to sell British goods abroad.

But unemployment is also disastrous because it:
- makes people feel useless and unwanted.
- leads to social problems.
- is an economic waste because state benefits have to be paid.
- is a waste of human resources.

Unfortunately, it looks as if inflation and unemployment are linked:

rate of inflation	people unemployed
25%	half a million
20%	1 million
15%	1¼ million
10%	2 million
5%	3 million
0	4 million

If you were in a position of power, and you had to decide on one of the combinations given above, which one would you choose?

It looks as if inflation can only be controlled through higher unemployment. But economists (who often have very different opinions) can't decide if this is true. In any case, there are many people who argue that governments cannot stand aside from unemployment. They must do *something*. So, in the 1970s and 1980s, there have been many different policies to try to get people back to work. These have included:
- grants to industry to build factories in areas of high unemployment.
- grants to exporting companies.
- help to people who start up new businesses.
- training schemes for young people and for redundant workers.

Under control . . . or not?

We began this section of the book by asking how governments control the economy. You should now know some of the answers.

They do it by regulating the amount of money in circulation. They do it by offering incentives to industry. They do it by fixing import and export duties, by joining the EEC (the European Economic Community which has enlarged Britain's export market) and by controls on central and local government spending.

They exert this control through regulations, laws, the Budget, instructions to banks, agreement with foreign countries, money grants to industry and by all kinds of other controls.

Despite these policies, no government has yet been able to solve *all* the economic problems. For there are factors which cannot be controlled. Among them are changes in the *world economy*, to take only one example. As more countries such as those in the Middle East and North Africa have been able to produce and sell oil, the international price of oil has fallen. Britain, because of the oil finds in the North Sea, is now an exporter of oil. Falling prices means less money for the government.

In the early 1980s, too, there was a decline in *world trade*. Britain, like other manufacturing and exporting nations, suffered. These are factors which cannot be solved by Britain alone. It makes the problems of running the economy of Britain a very complex and difficult one, without easy solutions.

Assignment

In your notebook, explain in your own words the meaning of these words and phrases:
*balance of payments   inflation
   the money supply   unemployment*

30 Projects

The following are ideas for topics and subjects for projects, surveys and other coursework.

1. Think up a new product or a service. Plan a market research survey. This should contain an analysis of the market, ideas on how to reach it, and examples of the questions to be asked.
2. Study a manufacturing company. To do this properly will require at least one visit. Or better still spend some time in the company on a work experience or study project. The written work should contain details of products, management team, workforce, advertising and selling methods, and production.
3. Study a department store. This should include an analysis of the range of products, methods of advertising, sales organisation, customer reactions.
4. Study a trade union. Look at how it is organised locally. This should include interviews with shop stewards and the branch secretary or other local officials. Written work should describe negotiating procedures, how the union organises and holds meetings, and the services it provides for its members.
5. Study a department within either local government (the Housing Department, the Education Department etc), or the work of a central government department (such as the functions of the local Health and Social Security staff, a Jobcentre, or tax officials). This should be based on visits and conversations with officials.
6. Investigate some industrial relations case-studies. These will have to be researched, replacing real names with fictitious ones when producing written work. They could be based on the work of trade unions, companies or industrial tribunals, and might illustrate the rights and duties of employers and employees.
7. Plan an advertising campaign for a new product. This might involve design skills (in the preparation of layouts for brochures, catalogues and adverts), and should explain the objectives of the campaign as well as the means of carrying it out.
8. Set up a new business. Students should decide on the nature of the business or service, and describe (with plenty of examples) how the partnership or company is established, what it offers, how it will be financed, and how it will manufacture or provide goods or services.
9. Study briefly a large international company. This will have to be based on brochures, adverts and other materials most of which will be supplied by the company's promotional or information services. The survey should include financial details (turnover, profit, dividends etc), an analysis of the scope of its activities, locations, products and management.
10. Conduct a survey and analysis of industry in your local area. This should include maps showing the location and distribution of companies, describe regional employment policies, illustrate access by road, rail, sea and air, and analyse problems concerned with the contraction and expansion of industry and commerce in the area.

Business challenges

The best way of learning about business methods is to set up a *real* business. It is unlikely that this will be possible. The next best thing to do is to plan a business *as if it is real*.

This project has been designed so that groups of students, working in teams, can each plan to set up their own business using the following guidelines.

1. You have to think up a *business idea*. It could be to make and/or sell a product or to provide a service.
2. Next, the group has to plan, write and present a proposal for a potential financial backer. This should contain:
   - an outline of the idea.
   - an explanation of the market research planned, or what has already been done, and estimates of demand.

- an estimate of the labour supply needed.
- production plans.
- an outline of the marketing and sales plans, including an analysis of the competition.
- the financial requirements – how much money is needed and what it is for.
- the first year's budget.

3 Assuming that finance is now available, plan production, sales and distribution over a two-year period.

To do this properly, it is necessary to consult people who are in business. For example, it should be possible to approach a bank, a local advertising firm or an accountant for advice. Useful people might be found through the school or college's network of contacts.

Teamwork is essential. The team should be no more than six people. Different tasks could be given to members of the team.

4 Produce the final version in the form of a written explanation or Report, or by an oral presentation to the rest of the class, or by a video or other audio-visual method.

The report should contain evidence of the product (designs, drawings or a model of the article); evidence of careful thinking and planning; a good financial case for funding and for profits; evidence of local consultation; good marketing and selling ideas.

Index

Advertising, 43–5, 46–50, 53, 67–71
Agencies, 50
Automation, 38

Banking, 21–2, 25
Benefits, 108–9
Branch secretary, 80
British Standards Institution (BSI), 68
Brokers, 25–6
Business Expansion Scheme, 23

Capital, 21–2
Case-studies, 28–30, 58–9, 82–3
Chambers of Commerce, 85
Coal, 40
Companies, 8–10
Confederation of British Industry (CBI), 84–5
Conservation, 100–3
Consumers, 3, 67–71
Consumers' Association, 70
Costs, 18–19, 58
Credit, 70
Customers, 33, 66

Debentures, 26
Demand, 62–3
Department of Trade and Industry (DTI), 23
Design, 65
Design Centre, 68
Discount stores, 56
Dismissal, 75
Distribution, 45
Dividends, 26

Employee participation, 86–91
Employment, 72–7, 78–83, 86–7
Employment law, 74–5
Energy, 33, 100–2
Engineering, 22
Enterprise Allowance Scheme, 23
Equal opportunities, 76
Equities, 26
Esso, 61

Factories, 38–9, 81–2
Fair trading, 67–8
Finance, 65
Finance Act, 97
Forming a business, 7–8

Gilts, 27

Health and safety, 75
Heavy industry, 39
Hire purchase, 70
Hypermarket, 55

Income tax, 107
Industrial design, 14–15
Industrial tribunal, 76
Industry, 1–5, 32–3, 35–7, 39–41
Inflation, 10–11
Institute of Directors, 85

Jobs, 72–4

Labour, 20, 33, 78–80
Launch, 43–4
Light industry, 40
Local government, 94–8
Location of industry, 32–5

Mail order, 56–7
Manufacturing industry, 35–7, 52–3
Marketing, 15–17, 43–5, 66
Market research, 15–17
Marks & Spencer, 58–9
Media, 50–1
Microcomputers, 13
Money, 21–3
Multinational companies, 39, 60–1
Multiple stores, 54

National insurance, 107
Nationalised industry, 93
New technology, 38–9
Nuclear power, 102

Partnership, 8
Pay, 75–6
Personal incomes, 106–7
Peterborough, 34
Pollution, 100–3
Preference shares, 26
Press, 45, 51
Pricing, 18–20, 62–4
Private enterprise, 92
Private industry, 8
Production, 32–4, 41
Profit, 18–20, 64–5
Prospectus, 27
Public limited company, 10, 24–7
Public relations, 44–5

Public sector, 92
Public spending, 96-7

Redundancy, 75-6
Registration, 9
Research and development, 13-14
Retailer, 52-6
Rights at work, 72

Sales, 19-20, 43-5, 52-4, 65
Service industry, 3
Shares, 10, 25-7
Shipbuilding, 39
Shop steward, 80
Sick pay, 75
Small business, 6-7
Small Firms Service, 23
Sole trader, 7
Special development areas, 34, 50
Standards, 69
Steel industry, 40

Stock Exchange, 25-7
Supermarkets, 55
Supply, 62-3

Taxes 97, 107-8
Tolpuddle, 79
Trade Union Congress (TUC), 81
Trade unions, 78-83
Trades Descriptions Act, 67-8
Training, 72-4
Transport, 40
Turnover, 64-5

Unemployment, 112-3

Value Added Tax (VAT), 107
Value analysis, 64
Venture capital, 23

Which?, 70
Wholesalers, 52-3